WORKBOOK

Environmental Studies

1

WORKBOOK

Environmental Studies

1

Manisha Malhotra

ARIHANT PRAKASHAN SERIES, MEERUT

WORKBOOK Environmental Studies 1ˢᵗ

ARIHANT PRAKASHAN SERIES, MEERUT
ALL RIGHTS RESERVED

卐 **Administrative & Production Offices**

Regd. Office:

'Ramchhaya' 4577/15, Agarwal Road, Darya Ganj, New Delhi -110002
Tele: 011- 47630600, 43518550; Fax: 011- 23280316

卐 Head Office:
Kalindi, TP Nagar, Meerut (UP) - 250002
Tele: 0121-2401479, 2512970, 4004199; Fax: 0121-2401648

卐 **Sales & Support Offices**

Agra, Ahmedabad, Bengaluru Bareilly, Chennai, Delhi, Guwahati, Hyderabad,
Jaipur, Jhansi, Kolkata, Lucknow, Meerut, Nagpur, Pune & Patna

卐 **ISBN :** 978-93-13198-02-4

卐 **Price :** ₹ 80.00

PUBLISHED BY : ARIHANT PUBLICATIONS (INDIA) LIMITED

Publishing Manager	:	Mahendra Singh Rawat, Keshav Mohan	Layout & Design	:	Pradeep Kumar
			Front Page Designers	:	Ravindra Kumar, Krishan Saini
Project Manager	:	Karishma Yadav	Proof Reader	:	Renu Sonkar
Project Coordinator	:	Divya Gusain	Figure Illustrator	:	Deepa, B.P. Singh
Cover Design	:	Aas Mohammad Malik			

For further information about the products from Arihant
log on to www.arihantbooks.com or email to info@arihantbooks.com

PREFACE

This Workbook, through its numerous exercises having different **variety of questions** will prove to be equally useful for both, **Classroom** and at **Home**. One more purpose of this Workbook is to provide the students a **systematic practice** of the content taught in the class and what they study in the textbooks.

Some special features of this Workbook are

- Different variety of questions; Fill in the Blanks, Picture Based Questions, Matching, Fun Activities, etc.

- Many questions given in each chapter are related with day-to-day activities making them interesting.

- Keeps the students actively engaged with the content and develop enquiry skills.

All the material given in this Workbook is tailored to suit subject content with equal support on learning, which will surely help students to boost their abilities and confidence in the subject.

I look forward for the feedback from students, teachers and parents for the further improvement of the contents of this book. I will try to update the contents according to your feedback in further editions of this Workbook.

The Publisher

CONTENTS

01

About Myself

1. Answer the following questions.

(a) My name is _______________________________ .

(b) My birthday comes on _______________________ .

(c) I am _______________________________ years old.

(d) I am a Girl [ ] / Boy [ ]

(e) I am studying in class _______________________ .

(f) The name of my school is _____________________ .

(g) My best friend is ___________________________ .

(h) My favourite food is ________________________ .

(i) My favourite cartoon is ______________________ .

(j) The name of my country is ____________________ .

(k) The name of my city is _______________________ .

2. Write the first alphabet of your name.

____

3. Write the name of your class teacher.

____

Fun Activity

1. Join the dots and complete the picture of flower.

2. Paste the picture of your best friend.

02

About My Body

My Body Parts

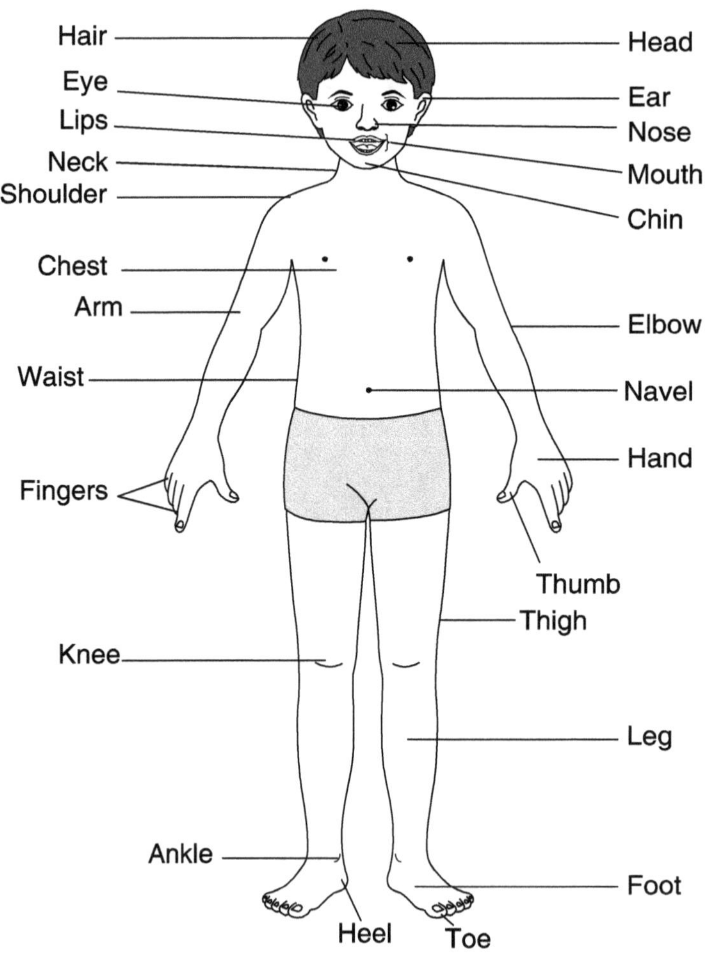

Exercise

1. Identify and mark the body parts in the given face with the help of words given in the box.

| Hair | Eye | Ear | Lips | Nose |

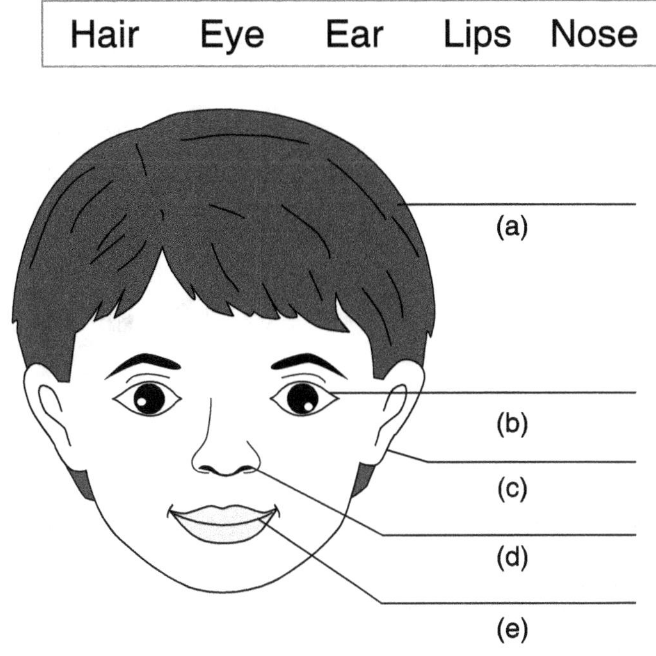

(a)

(b)

(c)

(d)

(e)

2. Tick (✓) the correct one.

(a) I have (one ☐ /two ☐) nose.

(b) I have (five ☐ /six ☐) fingers.

(c) I have (one ☐ /two ☐) mouth.

(d) I write with my (hands ☐ / ☐ foot).

3. Fill in the blanks with the help of words given in the box.

| Ears | Tongue | Eyes | Mouth |

(a) I hear with my ___________________ .

(b) I taste food with my ___________________ .

(c) I eat with my ___________________ .

(d) I see with my ___________________ .

4. Identify the body parts.

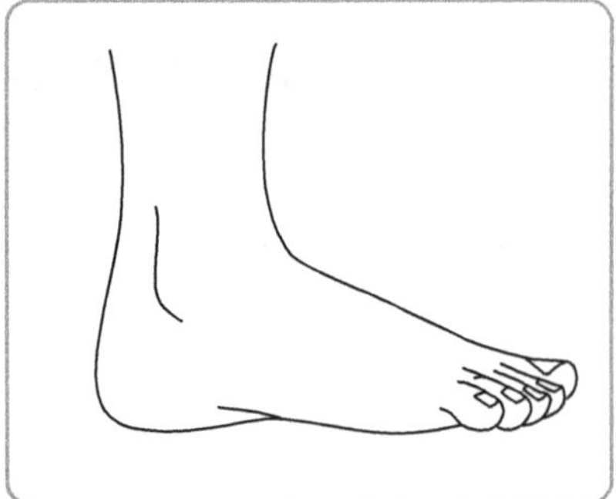

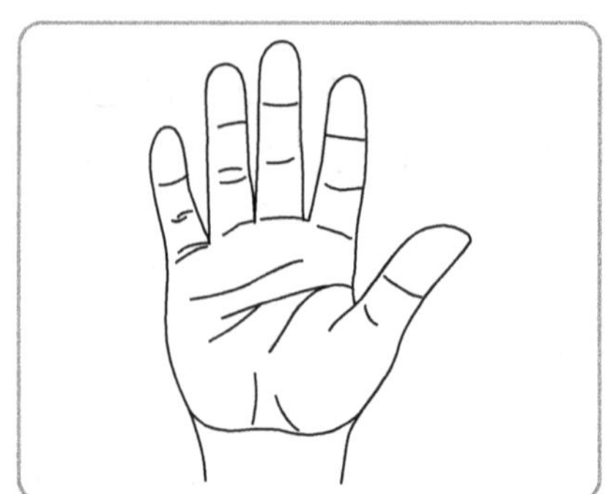

(a) This is my________________ .　　(b) This is my________________ .

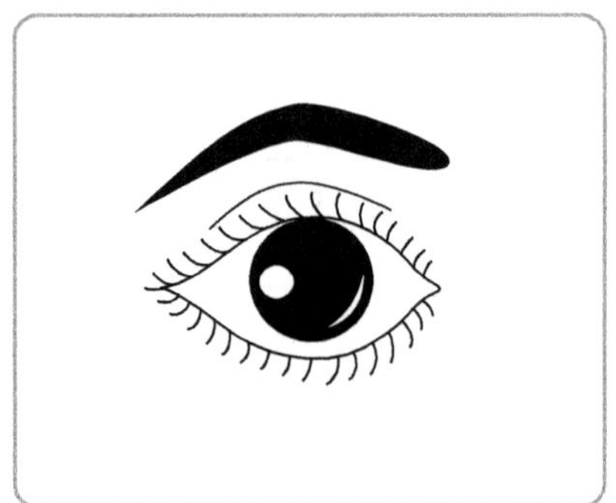

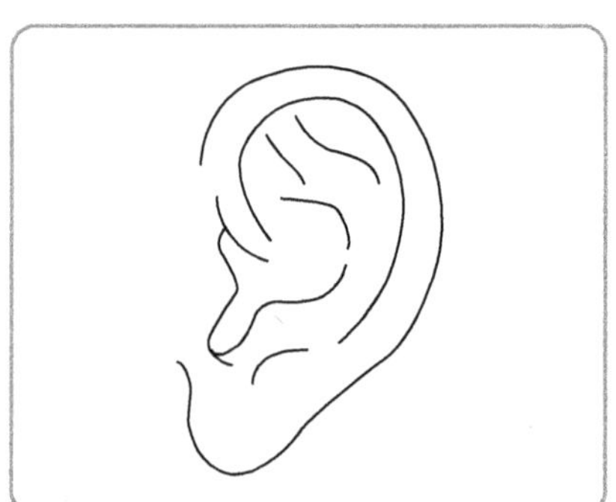

(c) This is my________________ .　　(d) This is my________________ .

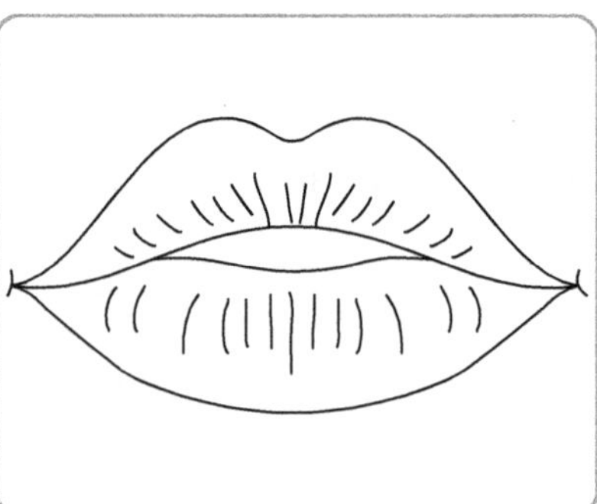

(e) These are my ________________ .

Fun Activity

- Join the dots and colour the body of this cartoon.

03

My Sense Organs

- I have five sense organs.
- They help me in seeing, hearing, smelling, tasting and feeling.

I see around through
my eyes.

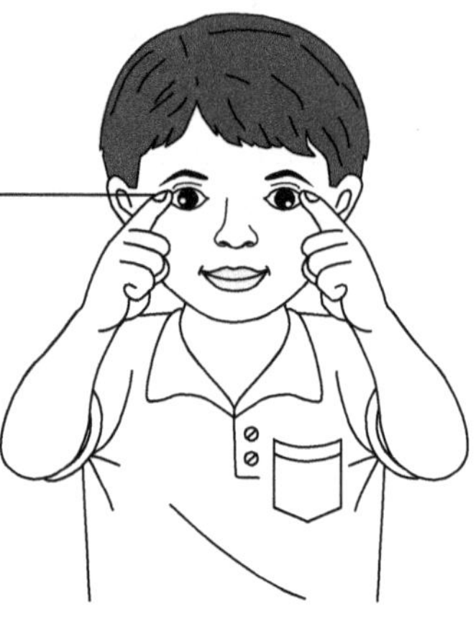

I can smell through
my nose.

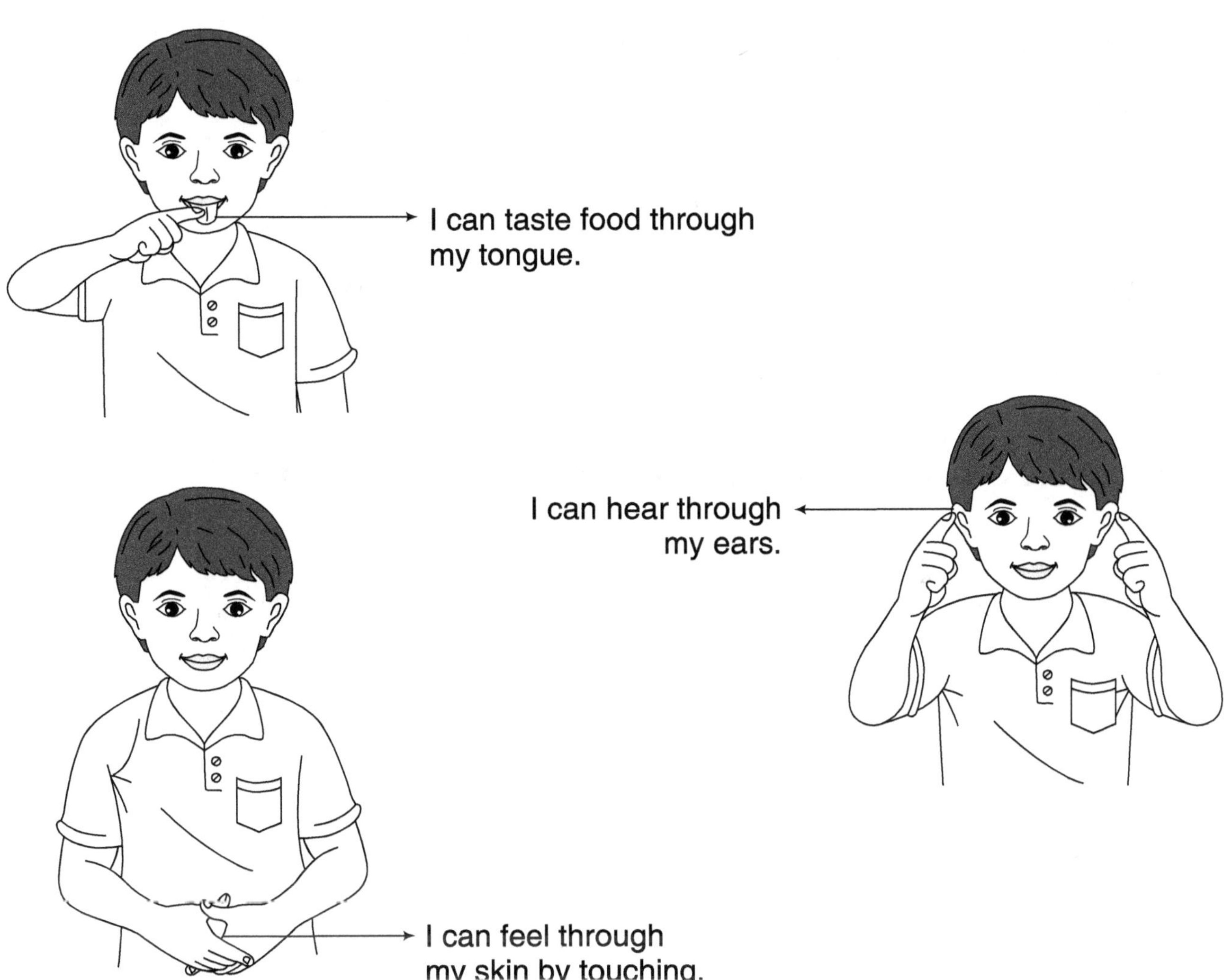

Exercise

1. Complete the sentences with the help of words given in the box.

| Skin   Tongue   Eyes   Nose |

(a) I can feel things through my ___________________ .

(b) I can see around through my ___________________ .

(c) I can smell flower with my ___________________ .

(d) I can taste food through my ___________________ .

2. Identify and circle ⬭ the five sense organs.

Legs	Foot	Eyes
Tongue	Stomach	Neck
Hair	Nose	Chest
Skin	Knee	Ears

3. Name the sense organs shown in the images given below.

(a) _______________________________

(b) _______________________________

(c) _______________________________

(d) _______________________________

(e) _______________________________

Fun Activity

- Colour this picture with your favourite colours.

Looking After My Body

I take bath everyday.

I brush my teeth twice a day.

I wash my hands before and after the meal.

I cut my nails once in a week.

I eat my meal on time.

I always sleep on time.

Exercise

1. Identify and tick (✓) the Toothbrush, Comb, Spoon/Plate and Clothes.

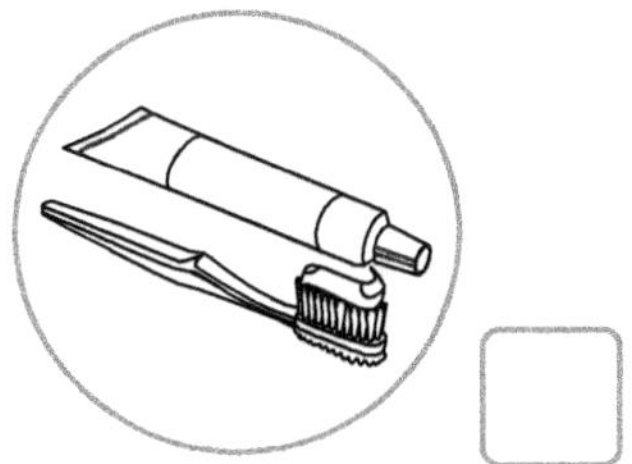  

  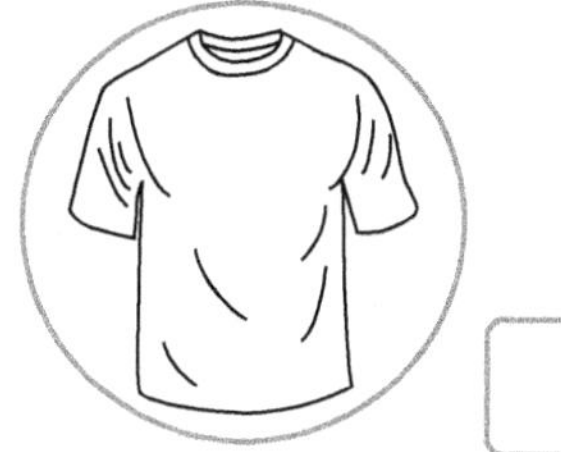

2. Answer the following in **Yes** or **No**.

(a) I wash my hands before and after the meal. _______________

(b) I brush my teeth everyday. _______________

(c) I take bath daily. _______________

(d) I wear dirty clothes. _______________

3. Complete the following sentences with the help of words given in the box.

Comb	Brush	Clean	Cut

(a) I ____ my hair daily.

(b) I keep my clothes ____ .

(c) I ____ my teeth twice a day.

(d) I ____ my nails once in a week.

Fun Activity

- Join the dots and colour the picture.

05

My Family

- Father, Mother and their Children form the family.
- Mother and Father are my parents.
- I live in a happy family.

What My Family Do For Me

My Mother prepares the meal for my family.

My Mother helps me in doing my homework.

My Mother gets me ready for the school.

My Mother looks after me when I am sick.

My Father takes me out for playing.

Exercise

1. Complete the following sentences.

(a) My family has ________________________________ members.

(b) Name of my Mother is ________________________________ .

(c) Name of my Father is ________________________________ .

(d) I have ____________ brother/brothers and ____________ sister/sisters.

(e) My Father's Mother is my ________________________________ .

(f) My Grandfather is my Father's ________________________________ .

2. Fill in the blanks with the help of the words given.

Care   Cooks   Problem   Playing

(a) My Mother takes ________________________________ of me when I am sick.

(b) My Father takes me out for ________________________________ .

(c) My Mother ________________________________ food for my family.

(d) My Father helps me to solve the ________________________________ .

3. Answer the following questions.

(a) What does your Mother do?

____

____

(b) What does your Father do?

____

____

Fun Activity

- Paste the photos of your family members and complete the family tree.

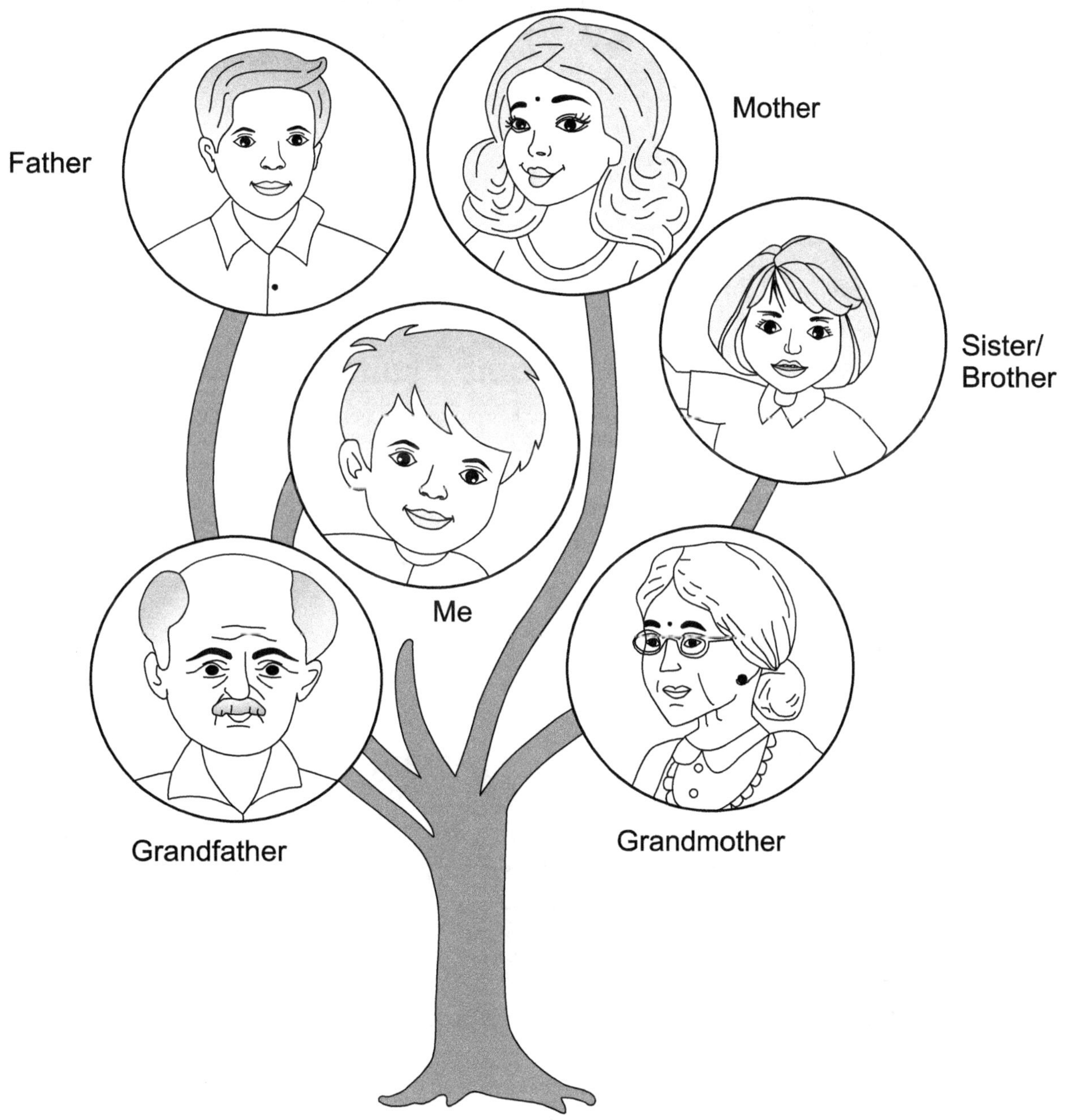

06

Food To Live

- We eat food to live.
- Food gives us energy.

Some Fruits

Apple

Banana

Guava

Mango

Orange

Pineapple

Some Vegetables

Carrot

Brinjal

Peas

Tomato

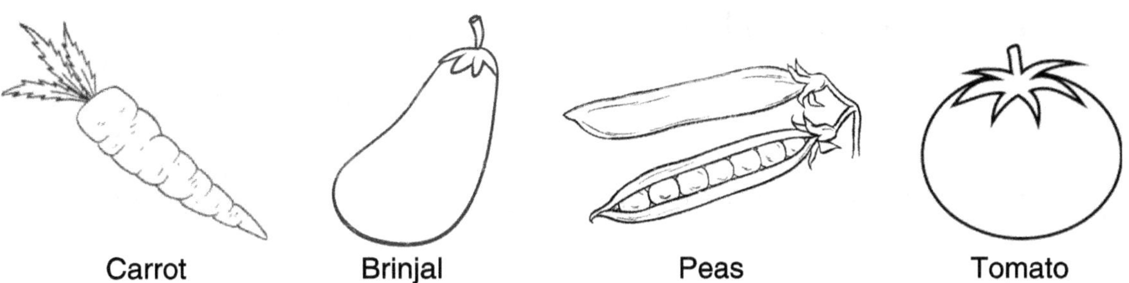

Exercise

1. Identify the fruits and vegetables in the given images and write their names in the given box.

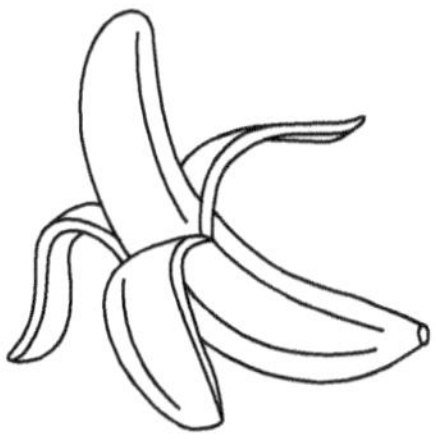

(a)

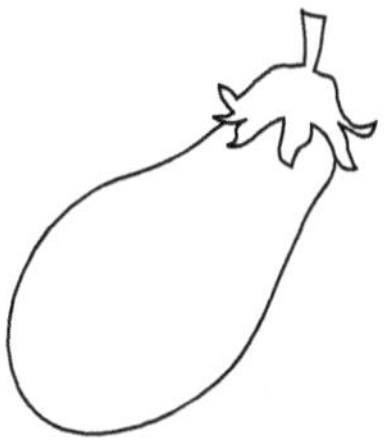

(b)

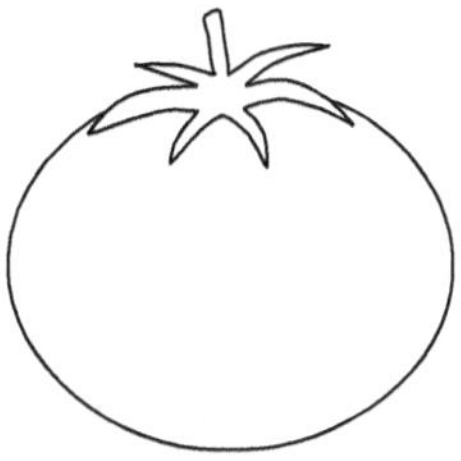

(c)

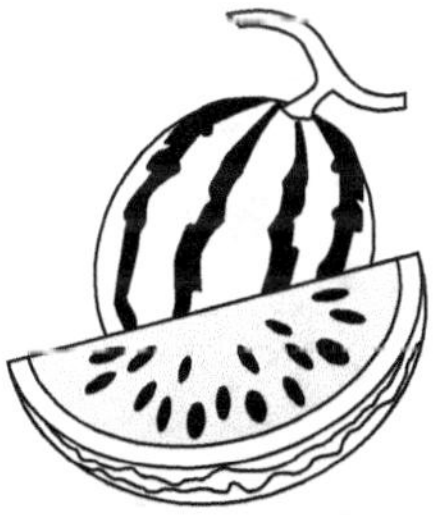

(d)

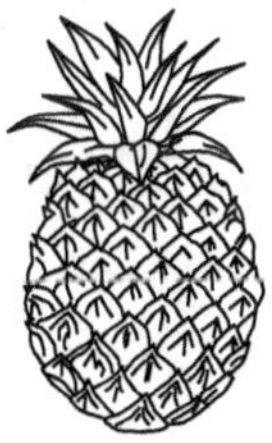

(e)

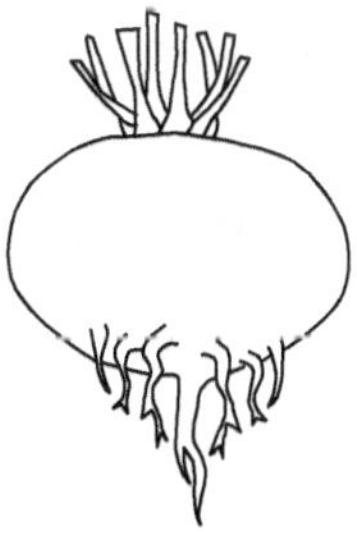

(f)

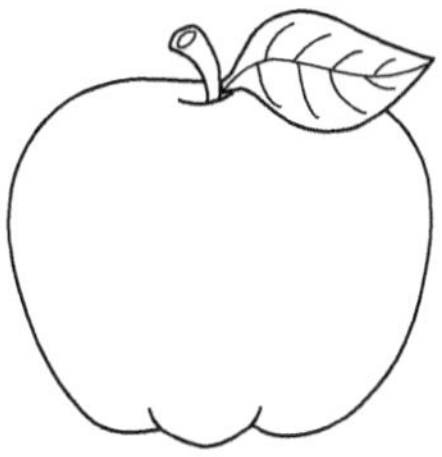

(g)

2. Answer the following questions.

   (a) Which is your favourite fruit?

   (b) Write the name of your favourite vegetable.

   (c) What is the colour of milk?

   (d) What time do you have your breakfast?

3. Give your answer in **Yes/No**.

   (a) We eat lunch every afternoon.

   (b) We eat dinner in the morning.

   (c) We wash hands before the meal.

Fun Activity

- Join the dots and colour the picture of Mickey Mouse.

07

Need of Clothes

- We wear clothes to cover our body.
- In winter, clothes keep us warm.
- We need clothes to protect our body from dust, heat and cold.

WINTER CLOTHING

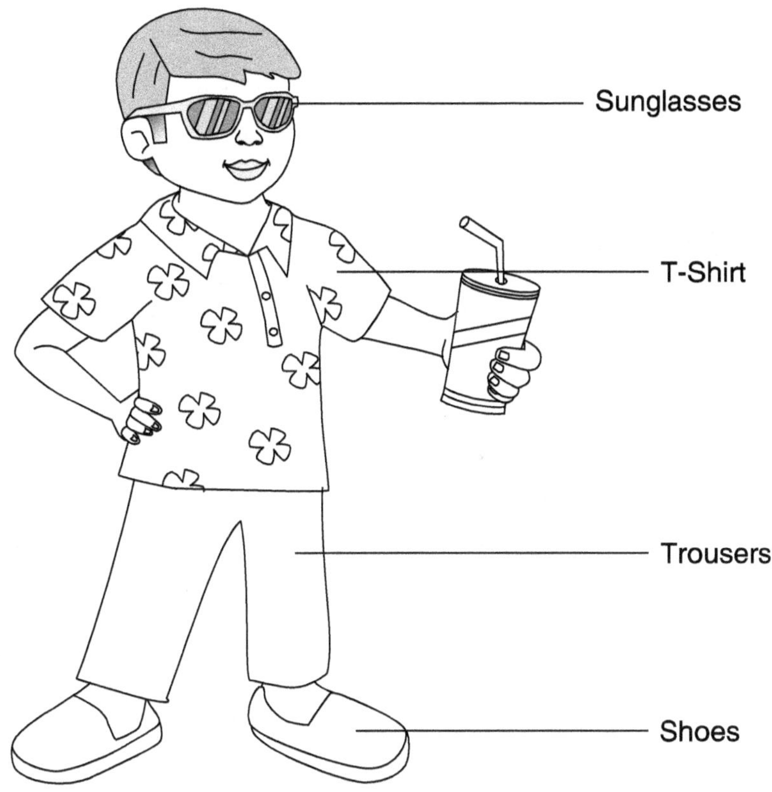

SUMMER CLOTHING

Exercise

1. Write the name of the clothes shown below with the help of words given box.

Cap	Gloves	Frock	Shorts
Trousers	Shoes	T-Shirt	Skirt

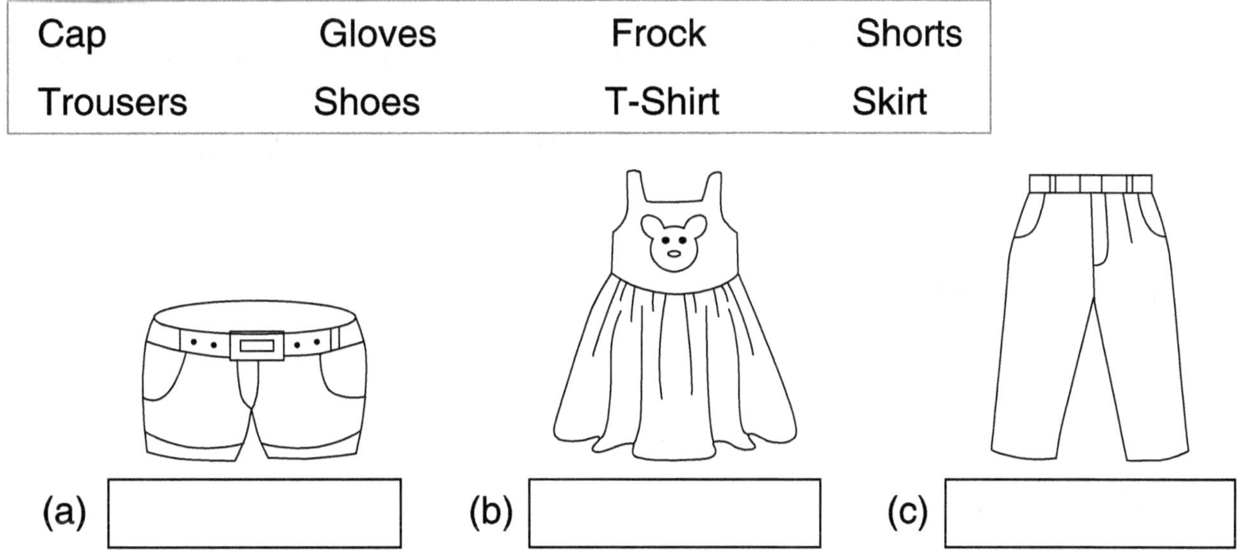

(a)   (b)   (c)

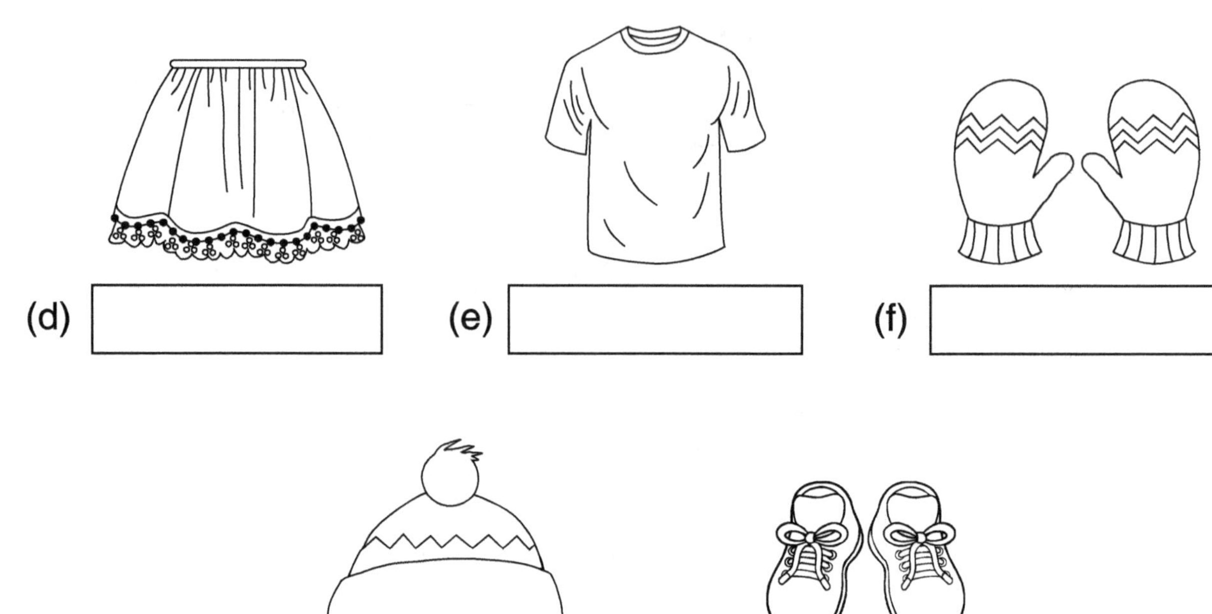

(d) [ ]   (e) [ ]   (f) [ ]

(g) [ ]   (h) [ ]

2. Fill the missing letters in the words given below.

(a) C__ O T__E__

(b) S H__ __ S

(c) __O C__ S

(d) G__ O__ E S

(e) C__P

3. Complete the following sentences with the help of words given in the box.

Feet	Head	Gloves

(a) I wear cap on my____ .

(b) I wear ____________________________________ in my hands.

(c) I wear socks in my____ .

Fun Activity

- Help the little girl to reach the shop through maze.

Home Sweet Home

- The place where we live is called home.
- It provides us safety and shelter.

Kutcha House [Mud House]

Pucca House [Brick House]

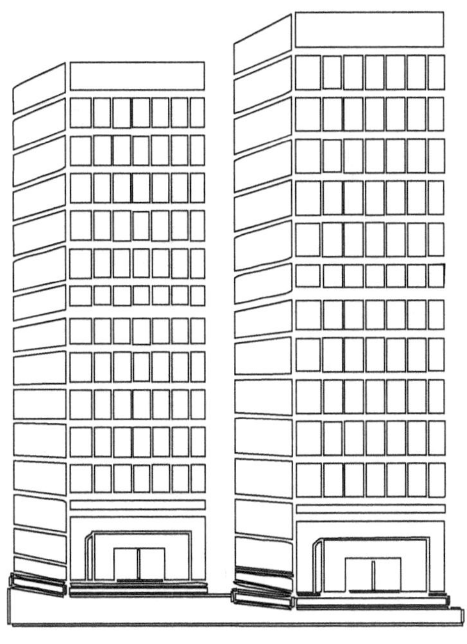

Building

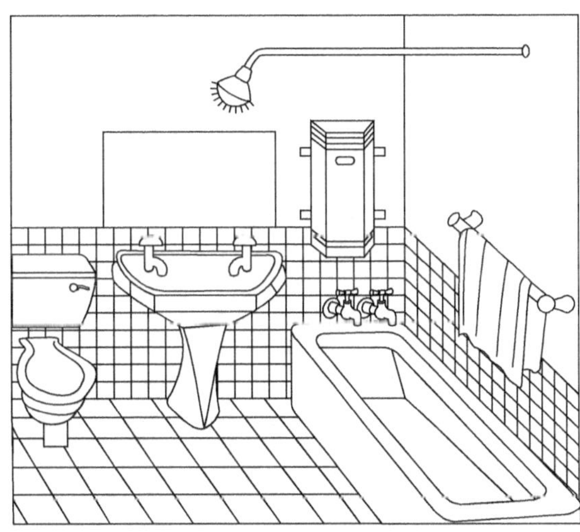

Bathroom

Bedroom

Kitchen

Drawing Room

Exercise

1. Complete the sentences.

(a) I live in a ____ house.

(b) My house has ____ rooms.

(c) The kutcha house is made up of _________________________ .

(d) The pucca house is made up of _________________________________ .

(e) Buildings are ____ .

(f) My mother cooks food in _____________________________________ .

(g) I take bath in ____ .

2. Match the following.

Category A   **Category B**

(a) I sleep in the   1. 

(b) Food is cooked in the   2. 

(c) I take bath in the   3. 

3. Fill in the missing letters and form the words.

(a) K __ T __ H __ N   (b) BE __ R __ __ M

(c) __ RAW __ N __ RO __ M   (d) B __ T __ ROO __

Fun Activity

- Join the dots and colour the happy house.

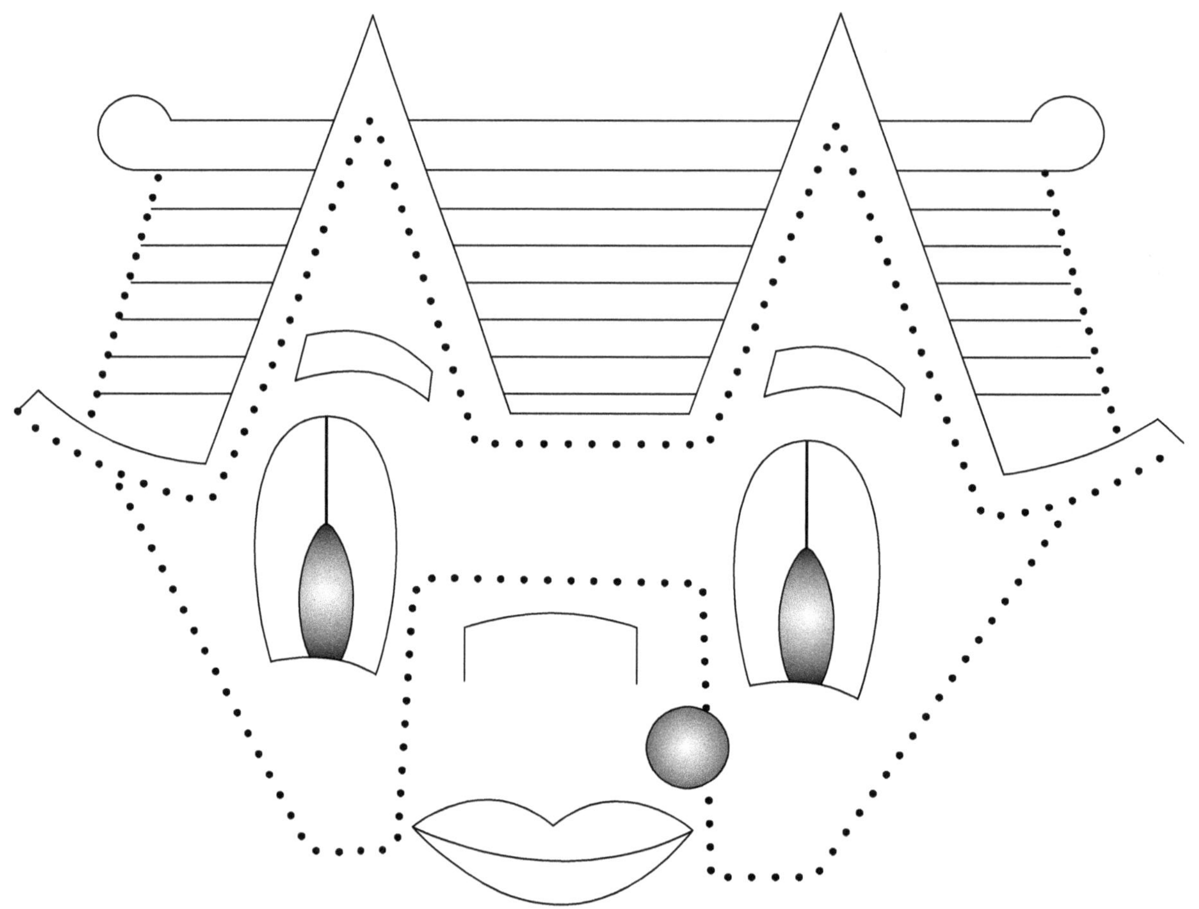

09

My School

- The place where I study is called school.
- My school has many children.
- It has many classrooms.
- My teacher teaches me good manners.
- I have many friends in school.
- I love going to school.
- Principal is the head of our school.

My Classroom

Exercise

1. Fill in the blanks with correct words.

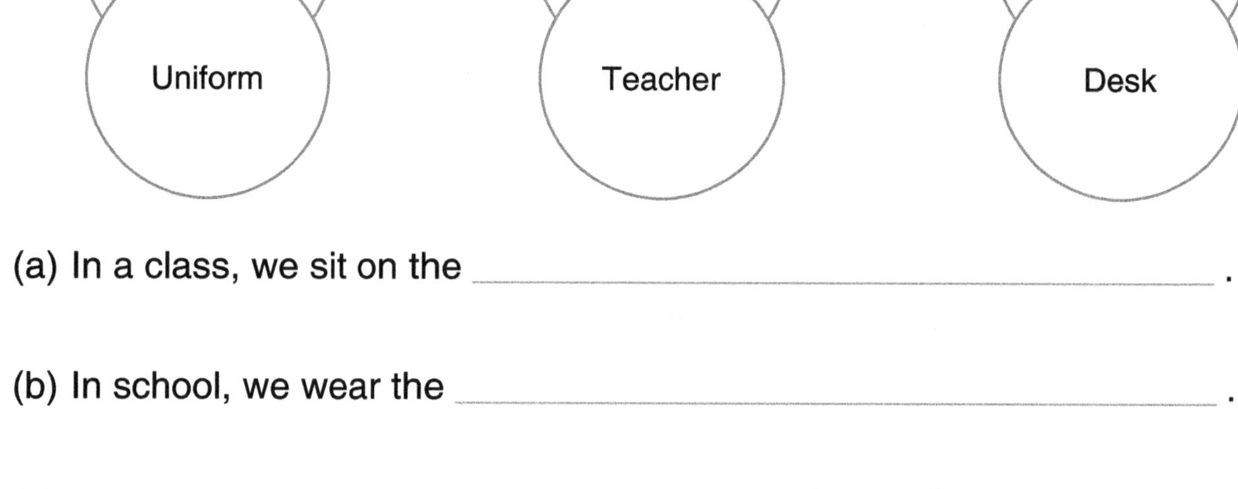

(a) In a class, we sit on the _______________________.

(b) In school, we wear the _______________________.

(c) _______________________ teaches us in the classroom.

2. Answer the following questions.

(a) What is the name of your school?

____

(b) In which class do you study?

____

(c) Who is your class teacher?

____

3. Fill in the blanks with the help of words given in box.

| Playground | Books | Classroom | Black Board |

(a) I study in _______________________________ .

(b) I study from the _______________________________ .

(c) I play in the _______________________________ .

(d) My teacher writes on the _______________________________ .

4. Match the following images with their names.

Category A   Category B

(a) 

1. Book

(b) 

2. Pencil

(c) 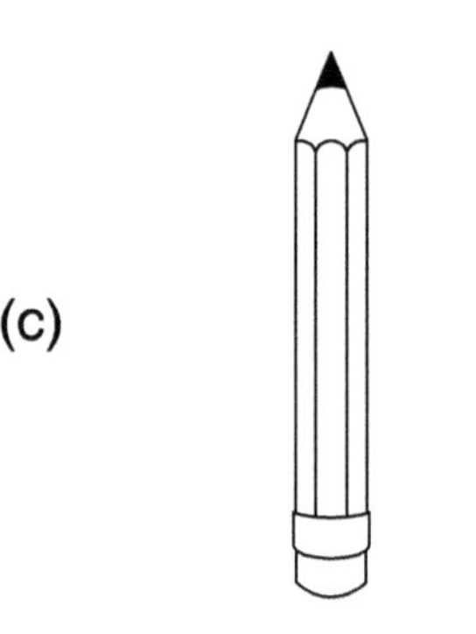

3. School Bus

(d) 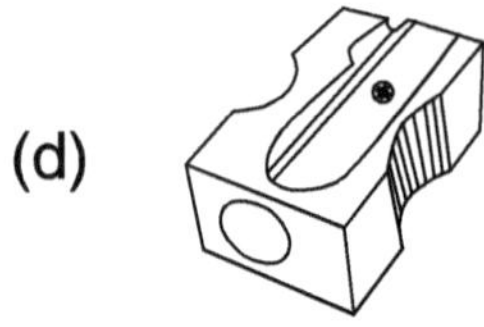

4. Sharpener

5. Write **Yes** or **No** against each sentence.

(a) I wish my teacher 'Good Morning' everyday. _______________

(b) I wear clean uniform in the school. _______________

(c) I comb my hair neatly everyday. _______________

(d) I share my lunch with my friends in the school. _______________

Fun Activity

- Draw the five things in the given boxes which you carry in your school bag.

10

Good Habits

We learn good habits in school and at home.

We should pray to God
before having our meal.

We should be kind to others
and should respect the elders.

- We should keep our surroundings clean.

- We should throw waste in the dustbin.

- We should wake up early in the morning.

- We should stand in a straight line (queue) and must wait for our turn.

Exercise

1. Fill in the blanks using the hints given in the box.

Thank you   Pray   Dustbin

(a) We should say _______________ when someone gives us something.

(b) We should _______________ to God before having our meal.

(c) We should throw waste in the _______________ .

2. Complete the following sentences with the help of words given in box.

Help   Early   Sleep   Queue

(a) We should get up _______________ in the morning.

(b) We should _______________ on time.

(c) We should _______________ others.

(d) We should stand in a _______________ .

3. Give your answer in **Yes** or **No**.

(a) I keep my clothes clean. _______________

(b) I help others. _______________

(c) I respect my elders. _______________

(d) I throw waste in my room. _______________

(e) I greet my teachers by saying 'Good Morning'. _______________

Fun Activity

- Colour the given picture of an aeroplane.

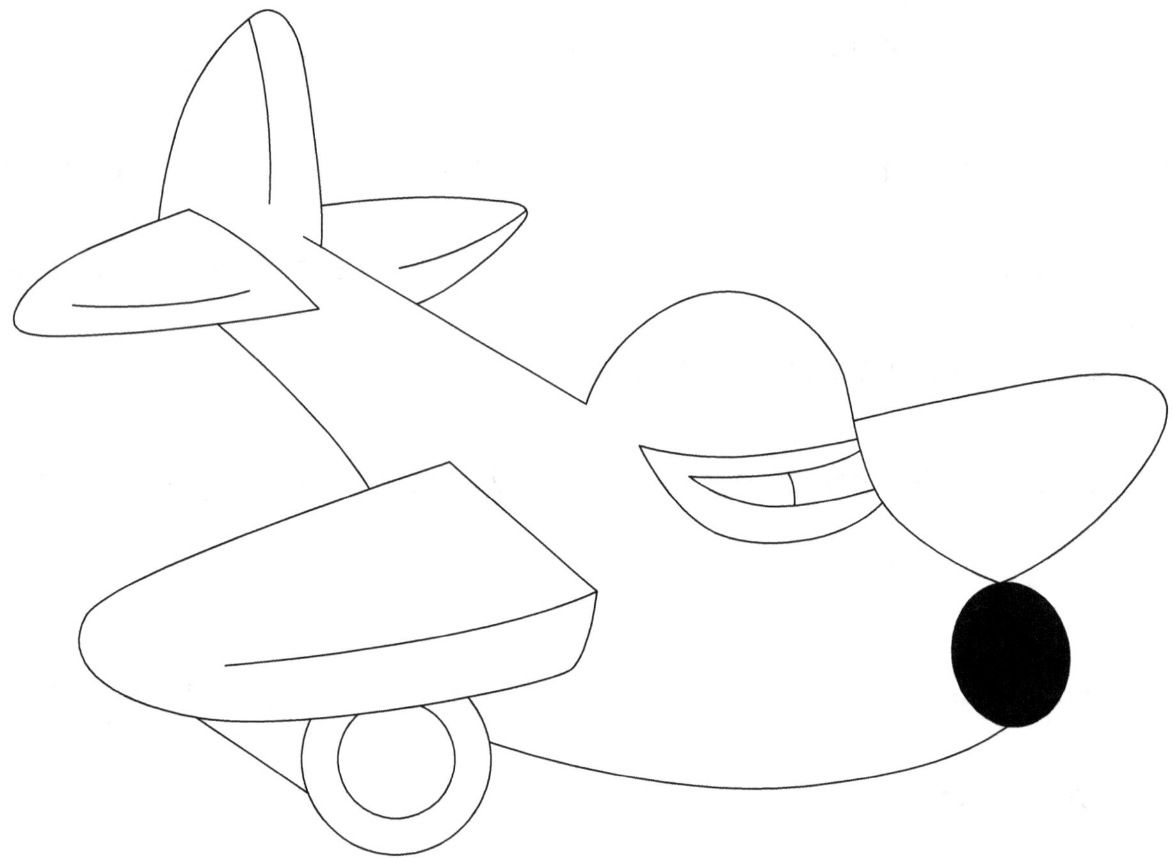

My Neighbourhood

- The places near my home is called neighbourhood.

- People living near my home are called neighbours.

- There are many houses in my neighbourhood.

- There is a park for children to play.

- There is a market to buy things.

- The people in our neighbourhood help us in the time of need.

People Who Help Us

Policeman
protects us from robbers and thieves.

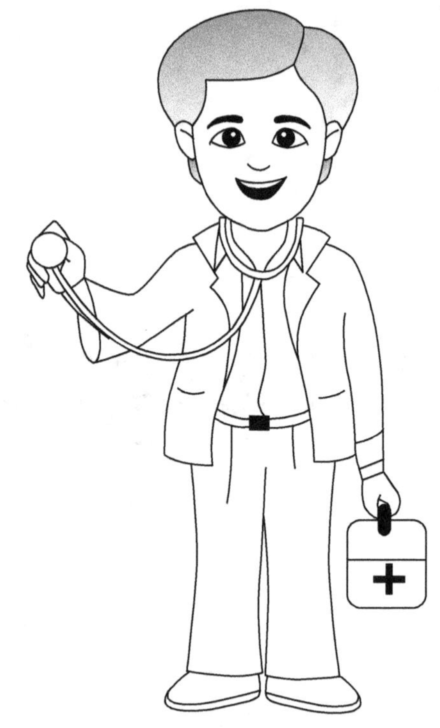

Doctor
gives us medicine when we are sick.

Fireman
extinguishes the fire
and rescue the people.

Mason
helps in building the house.

Tailor
helps in stitching our clothes.

Exercise

1. Fill the missing letters in the words given below.

(a) D___ CT___ ___

(b) PO___ IC___ M___ N

(c) F___ ___ E ___ AN

(d) ___ A ___ L ___ R

2. Fill in the blanks with the suitable words.

Park   Neighbours   Market

(a) The people who live near my house are my ________________________ .

(b) Children play in the ________________________________ .

(c) There is a ______________________________ to buy things.

3. Write the name of any three things that you find in your neighbourhood.

____

____

____

4. Match the following.

Category A	Category B
(a) 	1. Doctor
(b) 	2. Mason
(c) 	3. Postman
(d) 	4. Policeman

5. Fill in the blanks using the words given in the hint box.

| Stitching | Thieves | Building | Doctor |

(a) Tailor helps in ________________________ the clothes.

(b) Builder helps in ________________________ the house.

(c) ________________________ gives us medicine when we are sick.

(d) Policeman catches the ________________________ .

Fun Activity

- Join the dots and colour Chhota Bheem.

12

Festivals

- There are many festivals.
- We celebrate festivals together with joy.
- We cook special food during the festivals.
- Independence day and Republic day are our national festivals.

Diwali

- It is a festival of lights.
- People decorate their homes with diyas and flowers.
- We should not burst fire crackers.
- Fire crackers cause smoke and are bad for health.

Holi

- It is the festival of colours.
- People play Holi with colours.
- Many sweets are made during this festival.

Eid

- It is celebrated as a birthday of Prophet Muhammad.
- On this day, people go to Mosque to pray God.
- They wear new clothes and wish others Eid Mubarak by Hugging each other.
- They eat delicious sewaian and other sweets on Eid.

Christmas

- It is celebrated on 25th December of every year.
- Lord Jesus Christ was born on this day.
- People decorate their Christmas tree.
- Santa Claus brings gifts for the children on this day.

Lohri

- It is celebrated on 13th January of every year.
- The day after Lohri is celebrated as Maghi Sangrand.
- Lohri is celebrated with traditional dancing and singing around the bonfire.

Exercise

1. Fill in the blanks with the help of words given in the box.

| 15th August | 25th December | 26th January |

(a) Independence day is celebrated on _______________________.

(b) Republic day is celebrated on _______________________.

(c) Christmas is celebrated on _______________________.

2. Match the following.

Category A	**Category B**
(a) Festival of colours	Eid
(b) Festival of lights	Holi
(c) Sewaian	Diwali

3. Complete the sentences with the help of words given in the box.

(a) We cook special _____________ during the festivals.

(b) _____________________ is our national festival.

(c) We should not burst _____________________.

(d) People go to _____________________ on Eid.

| Mosque |
| Fire Crackers |
| Republic day |
| Food |

4. Circle the things that are associated with festivals.

Sewaian	Mosque	Diyas	Mango
Books	Shoes	Sweets	Flowers
Christmas Tree	Colours	Bags	Santa Claus

5. Answer the following questions.

(a) Which festival is known as 'Festival of Colours'?

____

(b) Which sweet is prepared on Eid?

____

(c) Who brings gifts on Christmas?

____

Fun Activity

- Colour the image of the diya for Diwali.

13

The Places of Worship

- The place where people worship God is called 'Place of Worship'.
- We worship God because he has created the world.
- God is one, but has different names like Krishna, Jesus, Allah, etc.

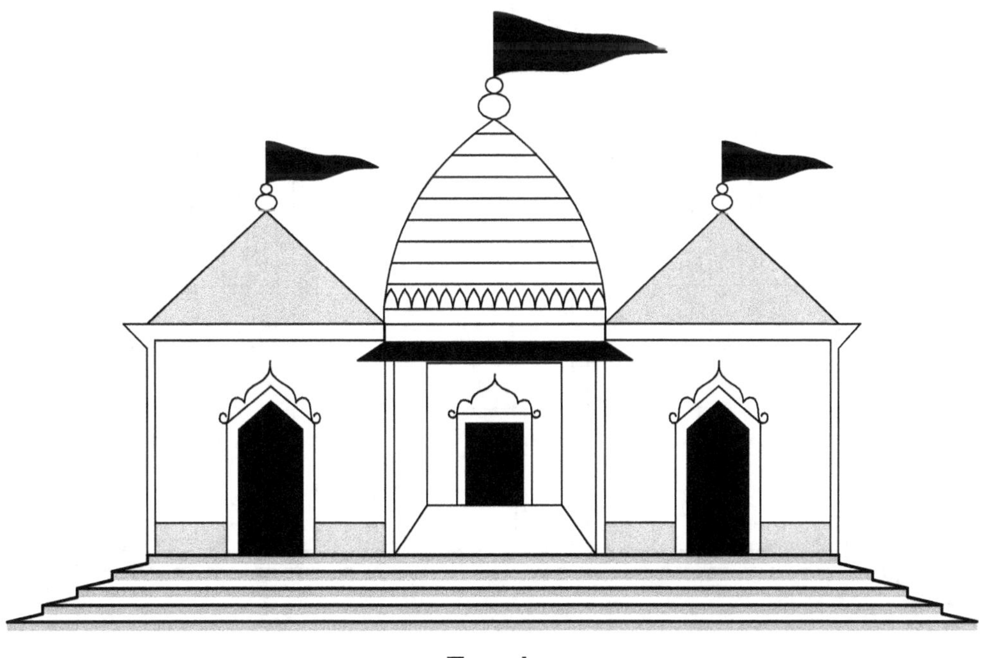

Temple

- Hindus go to temple to pray God.

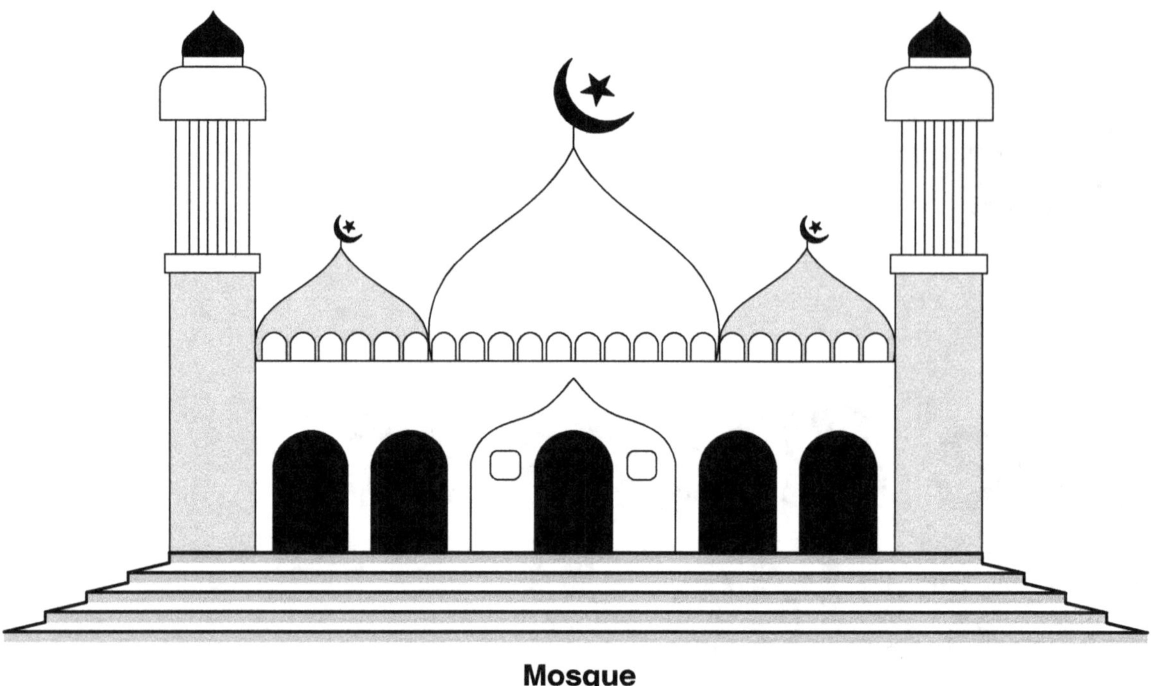

Mosque

- Muslims go to mosque to pray God (Allah).

Gurudwara

- Sikhs go to Gurudwara for prayer.

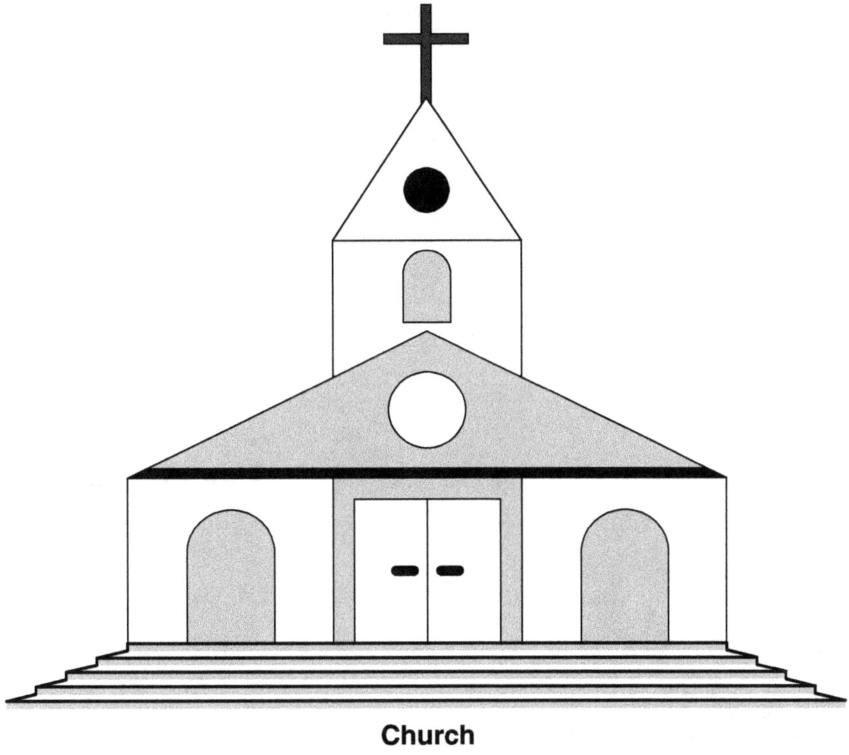

Church

- Church is the place of worship for Christians.

Exercise

1. Form the words from the jumbled-up letters given below.

(a) ODG ______________

(b) PAYR ______________

(c) ETPLEM ______________

2. Fill in the blanks using the words given in hint box.

| One | Church | God |

(a) The world is created by ________________________________ .

(b) Christians pray at the ________________________________ .

(c) There is ________________________________ God.

3. Complete the words given below by filling the missing letters.

(a) M ___ S ___ U E   (b) ___ E M ___ ___ E

(c) C ___ U ___ C ___

4. Match the following.

Category A   **Category B**

(a)    1. Christian

(b)    2. Sikh

(c)    3. Muslim

(d)   4. Hindu

Fun Activity

1. Paste the picture of a place of worship near your home.

2. Make the colourful body of the caterpillar with your favourite colour.

14

Safety Habits

- We should not play with fire,
  as it can harm us.

- We should use fire in the presence
  of an elder person.

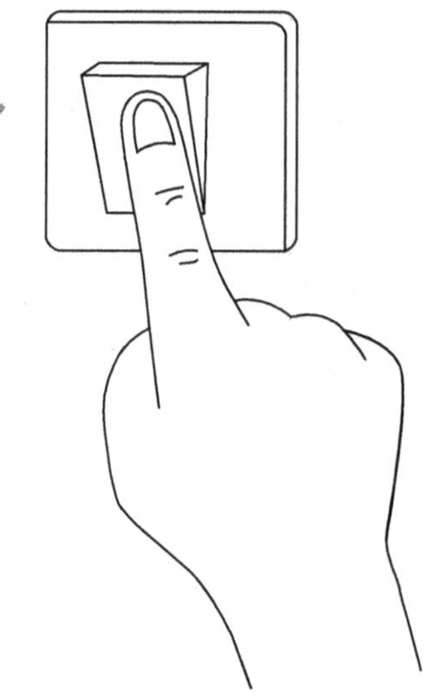

- We should not touch electric wires and should
  not play with switches.

- We should not take things from the strangers.

- Always play with your pet.
- Never tease the stray animals, as they can bite or scratch you.

- Never rush up/down a staircase.
- Never push someone on the staircase.
- Always take steady steps.

- We should not play with sharp objects.
- Scissors, knives, blades are the sharp objects.
- They may harm us.
- We should use them in the presence of elders.

Exercise

1. Complete the following sentences with the help of the given words.

Strangers   Fire   Rush

(a) We should not play with _________________________________ .

(b) We should never _____________________ up/down a staircase.

(c) We should never take things from _____________________ .

2. Give your answer in **Yes/No**.

(a) I never touch the switch with wet hands. _____________

(b) I never tease the stray animal. _____________

(c) I take things from the strangers. _____________

(d) I always take steady steps down the staircase. _____________

3. Write down the few safety habits that you follow at home.

____

____

____

____

____

4. Circle ◯ the objects given, which are not sharp.

Knives   Brush   Blade

Shoes   Scissors   Books

Fun Activity

• Colour the big fat cat to make it your pet.

15

Means of Transport

- People move from one place to another through means of transport.
- Bus, car, train, bullock cart, aeroplane, ship, boat— all are the part of means of transport.
- With the help of means of transport we reach our destination in less time.

Means of Transport on Land

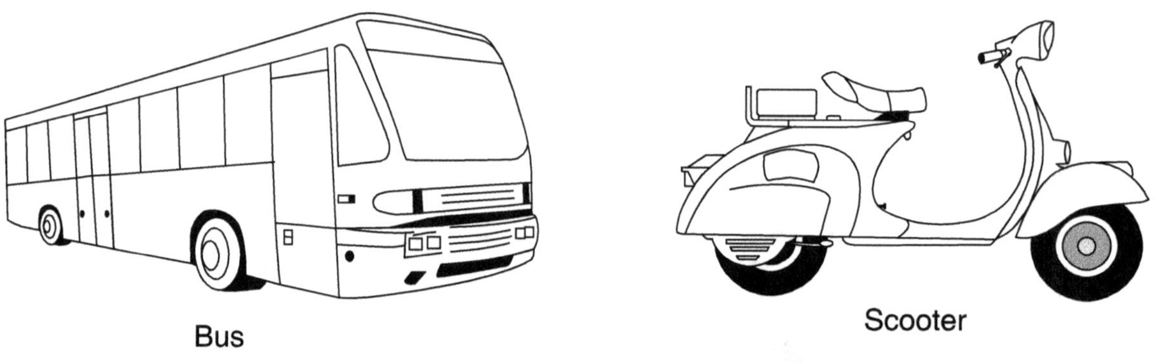

Bus

Scooter

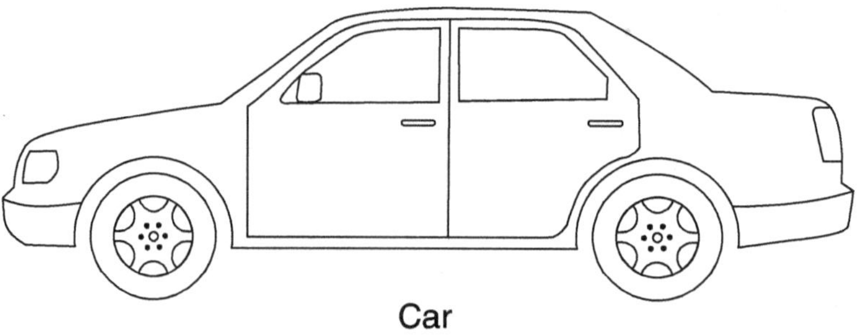

Car

Train

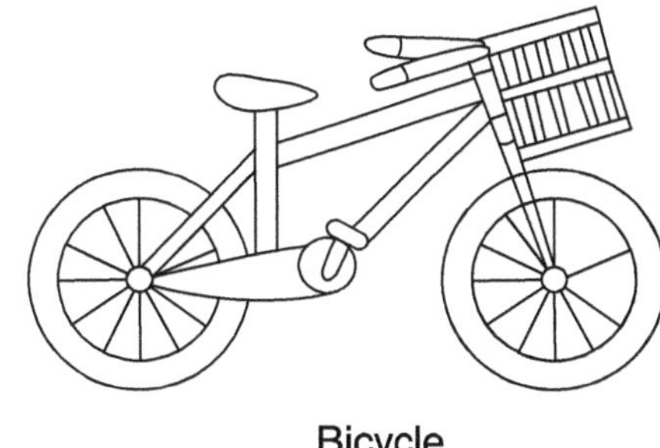

Bicycle

Means of Transport in Water

Ship

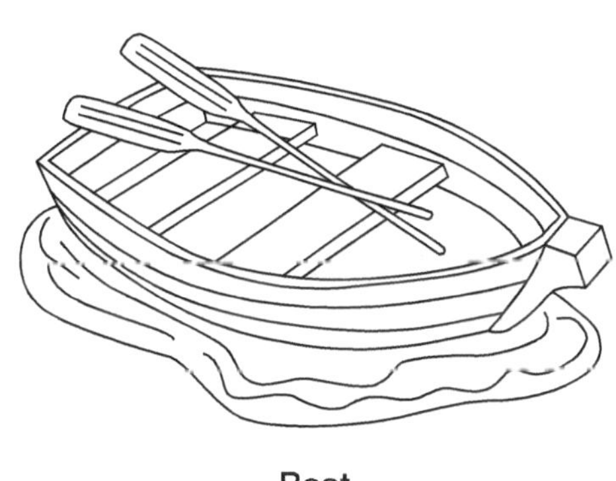

Boat

Means of Transport in Air

Aeroplane

Helicopter

Exercise

1. Complete the following words.

    (a) S ___ IP   (b)   A ___ R ___ P ___ A ___ E

    (c) B ___ A ___   (d)   ___ C ___ ___ TER

2. Write the answer of the following questions.

    (a) Name any one means of transport with two wheels.

    (b) Name the largest means of transport.

    (c) Name the slowest means of transport.

    (d) What are the two fastest means of transport?

3. Fill in the blanks.

    Air   Ship   Bus   Boat

    (a) _________________ is a form of road transport.

    (b) Aeroplane is a means of _________________ transport.

    (c) _________________ and _________________ are means of water transport.

4. Identify the following vehicles and write their names in the box below.

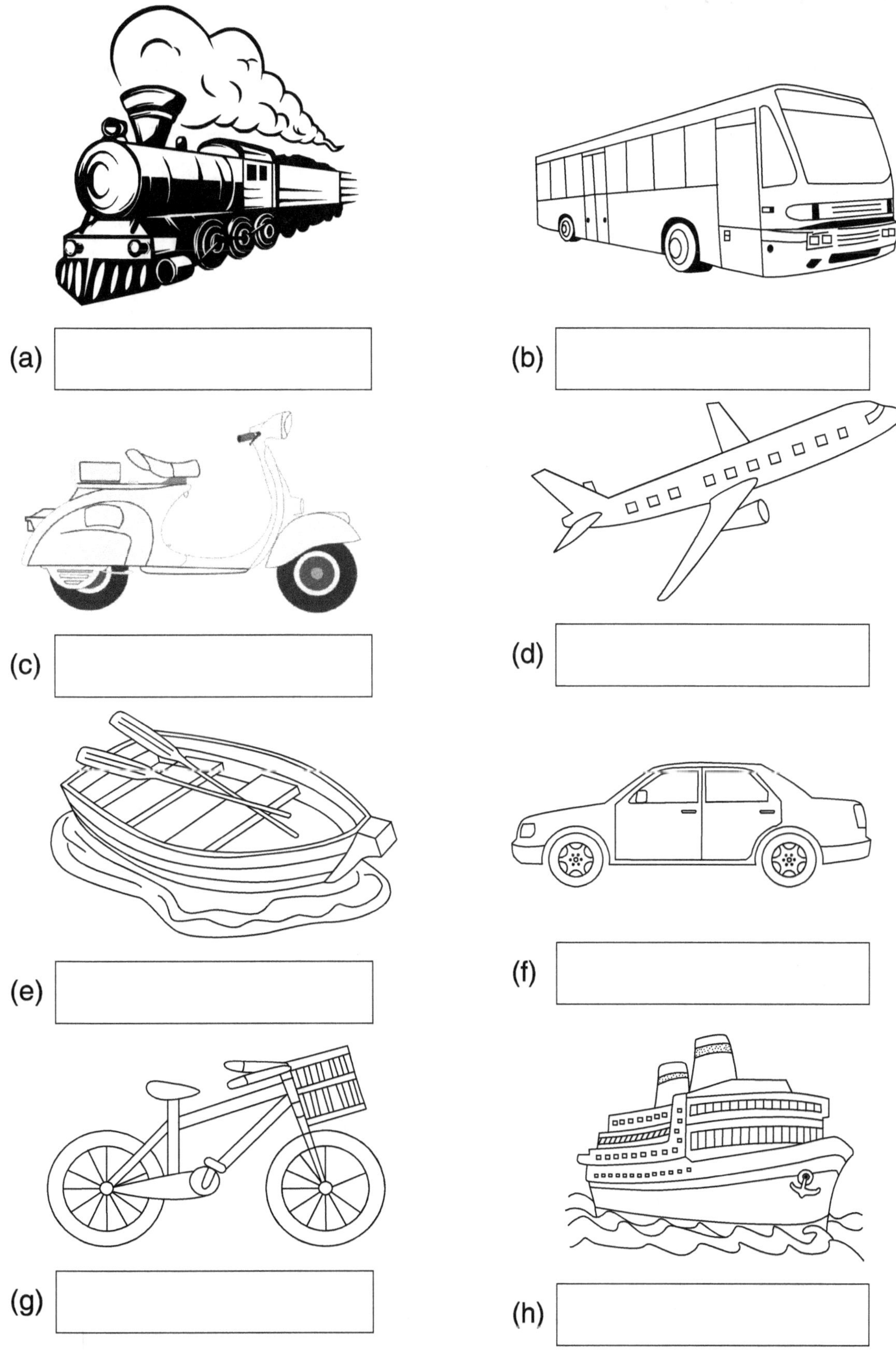

(a)

(b)

(c)

(d)

(e)

(f)

(g)

(h)

Fun Activity

- Paste the image of that means of transport which you use for going to school.

16

Road Safety

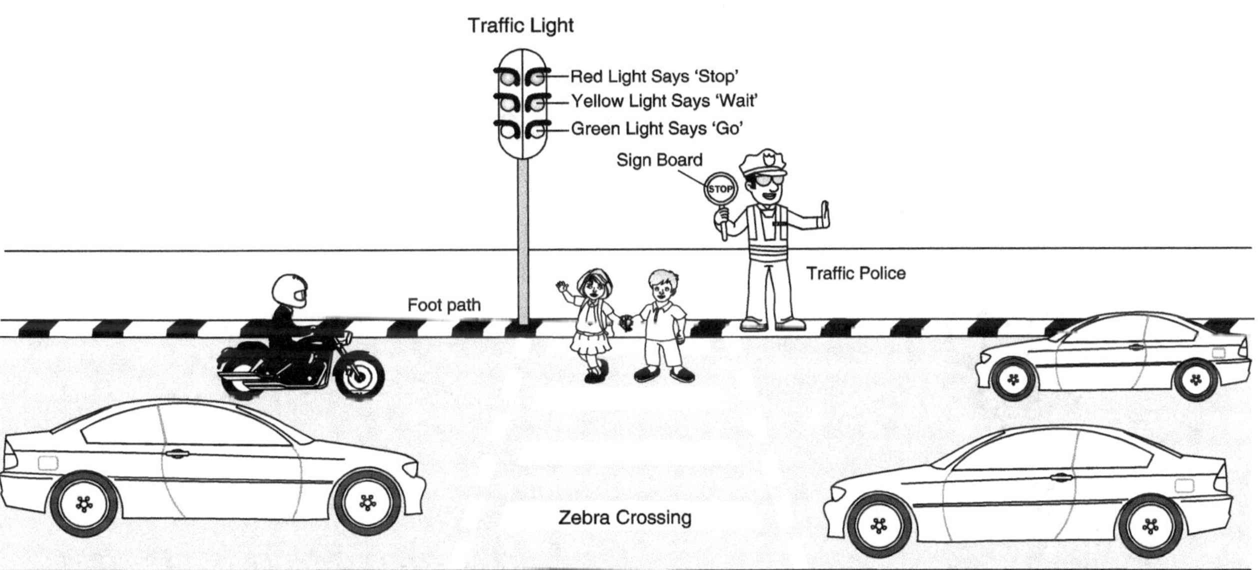

- Car, rickshaw, truck and bus are known as vehicles.
- They move on the road and create traffic.
- Traffic light is used for the safety of the people.
- It has three colours – Red, Yellow and Green.
- When it is 'Red', we must stop our vehicle.
- When it is 'Yellow', we must wait.
- When it is 'Green', we are ready to go.
- Traffic Police gives signals for movement of traffic.

Other Safety Rules

- We should always walk on the footpath.
- We should cross the road using zebra crossing.
- We should never try to get down of the moving bus.
- We should never play on the road.
- We should never run while crossing the road.
- We should follow the traffic light, traffic rules and sign boards.
- Before crossing the road, we should see right, then left and again right. If it is clear then cross the road.
- We should wear helmet while riding a bike.

Exercise

1. Match the following.

2. Fill in the blanks with the help of words given in the box.

| Run | Down | Footpath | Zebra Crossing |

(a) We should always walk on the ___________________________.

(b) Never ________________________________ on the road while crossing.

(c) Always cross the road using ________________________________.

(d) Never get ________________________ of the moving bus.

3. Give your answer in **Yes** or **No**.

(a) We should not obey the traffic rules.   ________

(b) I cross the road using zebra crossing.   ________

(c) We should wear helmet while riding a scooter.   ________

(d) Traffic light is for the safety of people.   ________

Fun Activity

- Draw an image of the traffic light (Red, Yellow and Green) using fingers by dipping them in colour.

Plant Life

17

- Plant grows out of a seed.
- It then becomes a big plant.
- It has leaves, flower, fruit, stem, roots and bud.
- Plants make their food using sunlight and water.

Parts of Plant

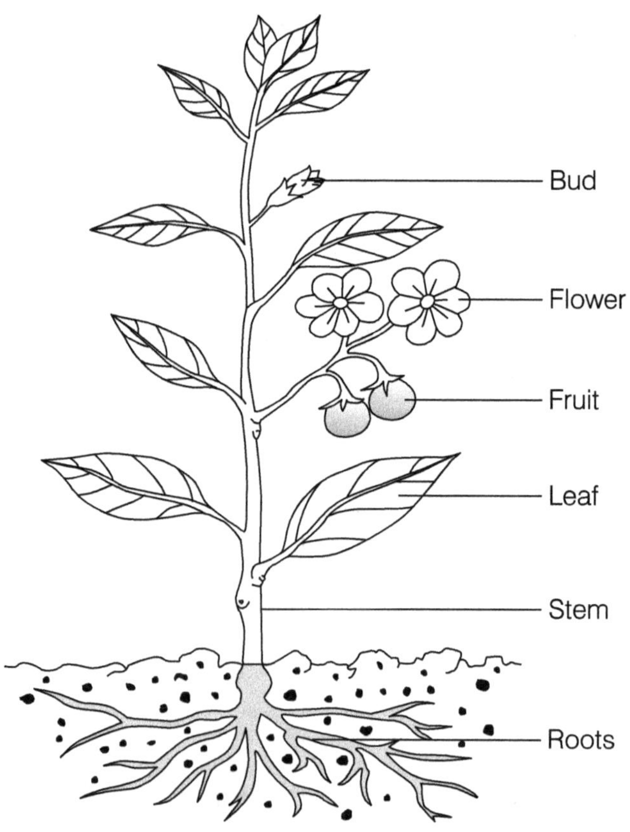

- We should water plants everyday.

- We should not cut the trees.

- Plants give us food, medicine and cotton.

- Plants keep the air fresh.

- Plants make our surroundings beautiful and green.

- We cannot live without plants. Therefore, we should plant more trees.

- Some trees are big and some are small.

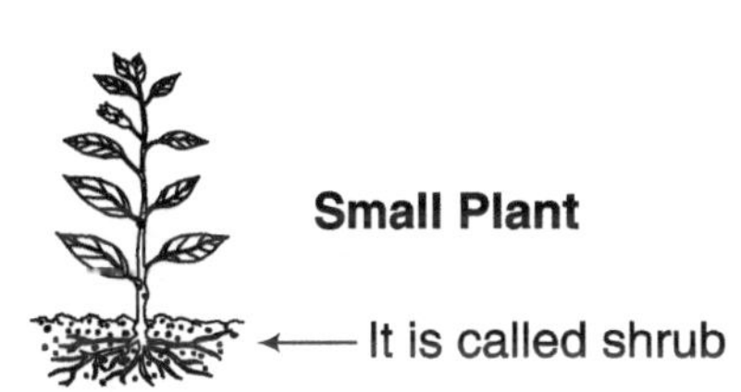

Exercise

1. Fill in the blanks with the help of the words given in the box.

Sunlight	Water	Air	Cut

(a) We should not ________________________ the trees.

(b) Plants make their food using ________________________ .

(c) Plants keep ________________________ fresh.

(d) We should ________________________ plants everyday.

2. Match the following.

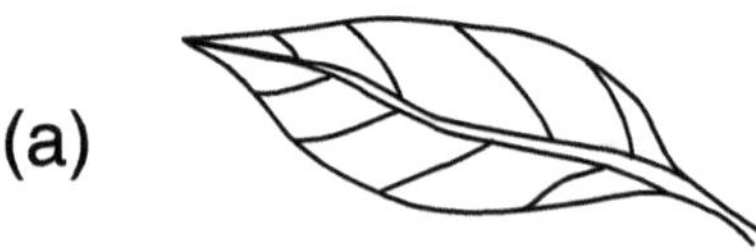

(a)   Flower

(b)   Leaf

(c)   Seed

(d)   Fruit

3. Answer the following questions.

(a) Big plants are known by which name?

____

(b) Small plants are known by which name?

____

(c) Why we should plant more trees?

____

4. Circle ⬭ the words which form the part of plant.

Flower	Clothes	Bud
Shoes	Fruit	Scissors
Leaves	Fan	Roots

Fun Activity

1. Complete the face of the fruit and colour it.

2. Collect the leaves of two different plants and paste them here.

18

Animals & Birds

- We see many animals around us.
- Animals like dog and cat can be made pets.
- Animals like lion, elephant and monkey live in jungle.
- Crocodile, duck and fish live in water.

- Birds live in nest.
- Birds fly in the sky. They are many types of birds like parrot and peacock.
- Cow and buffalo give us milk.
- Sheep gives us wool which is used for making warm clothes.

Loving the Animals

- Animals are harmless and our good friends.
- We should not harm the animals.
- We should love the animals.

Parts of Animal Body

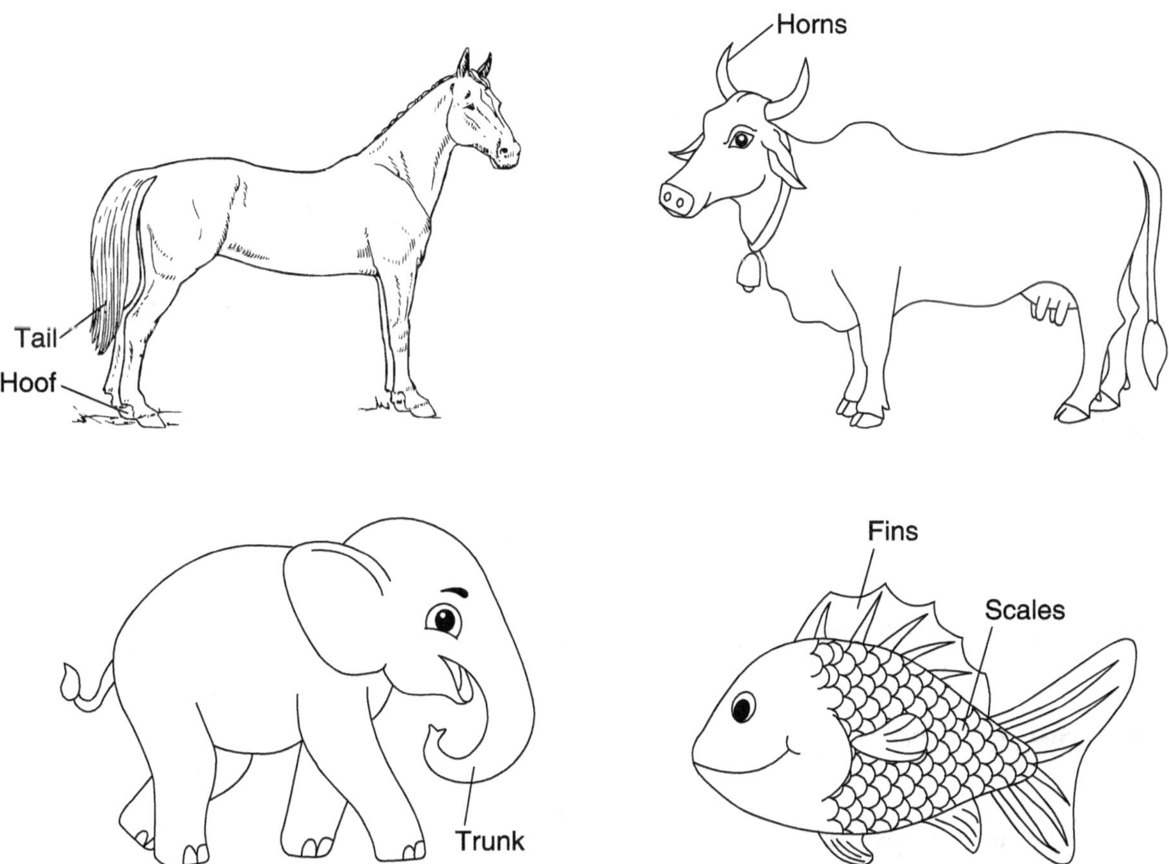

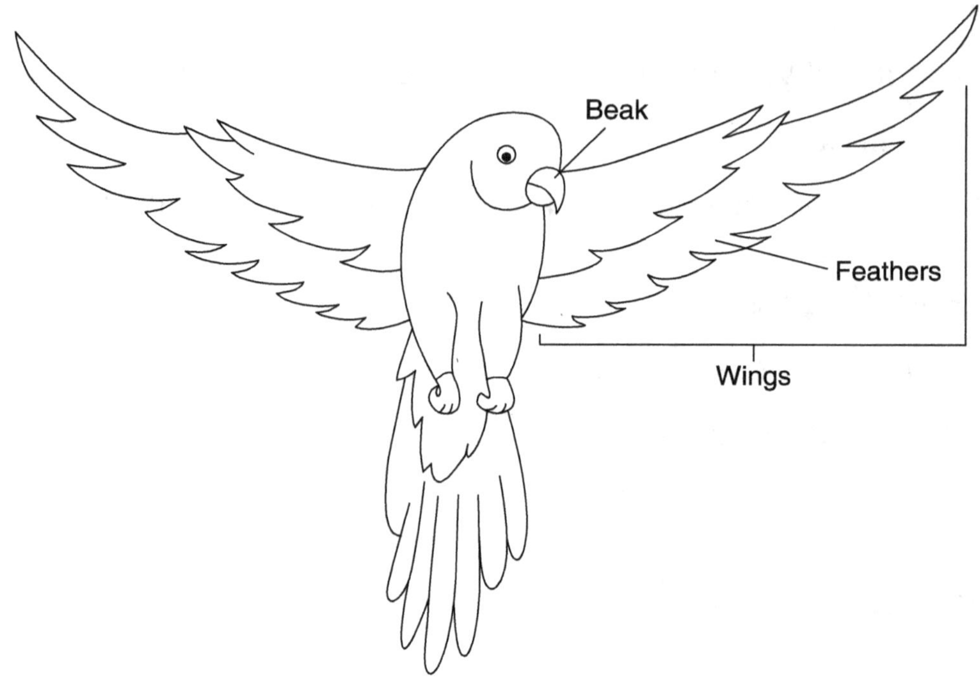

Exercise

1. Fill in the blanks with suitable words given in the box.

Trunk	Wings	Hoof	Horns	Fins

(a) Birds have _________________________ to fly.

(b) _________________________ help fish to swim in water.

(c) Nose of an elephant is known as _________________________ .

(d) Cow has two _________________________ .

(e) Feet of the horse is known as _________________________ .

2. Answer the following questions in **Yes** or **No**.

(a) Dog and cat can be made pets. _________

(b) Crocodile and fish live in water. ________

(c) Cow and buffalo give us milk. ________

(d) Sheep gives us cotton. ________

(e) We should harm the animals. ________

3. Match the following.

Home (Category A)   **Animals** (Category B)

(a)  Stable   1. Lion

(b)  Nest   2. Fish

(c)  Web   3. Bird

(d)  Jungle   4. Horse

(e) 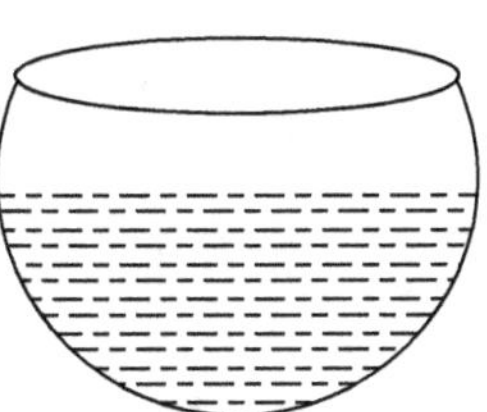 Water   5. Spider

4. Fill in the blanks with the help of words given in the box.

(a)   These are ________________ .

(b)   This is a ________________ .

(c)   These are ________________ .

(d)   These are ________________ .

(e)   This is a ________________ .

| Tail |
| Horns |
| Paw |
| Wings |
| Hooves |

Fun Activity

- Join the dots to complete the picture of Hello Kitty and colour it.

19

Our Mother Earth

- We live on planet Earth.

- Earth is round in shape.

- Major part of Earth is covered with water.

- Land is covered with plains and mountains.

Plain

Mountain

- Plains are a flat surface of land.

- Mountains are the high parts of land.

- There are many rivers on our Earth.

- These rivers contain water.

Directions

- There are four directions namely: East, West, North and South.

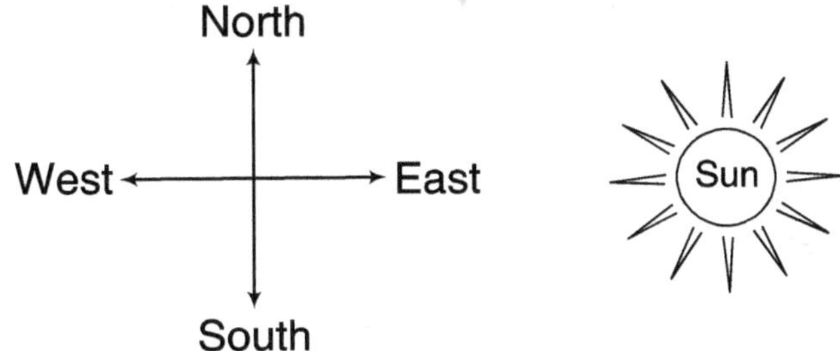

Exercise

1. Fill in the blanks.

(a) Earth is _______________________ .   Square/Round

(b) Mountains are _______________________ .   Low/High

(c) Rivers contain _______________________ .   Snow/Water

(d) There are _______________________ directions.   Five/Four

(e) The Sun rises in the _______________________ .   East/West

(f) The Sun sets in the _______________________ .   North/West

2. Name the directions in the box given box.

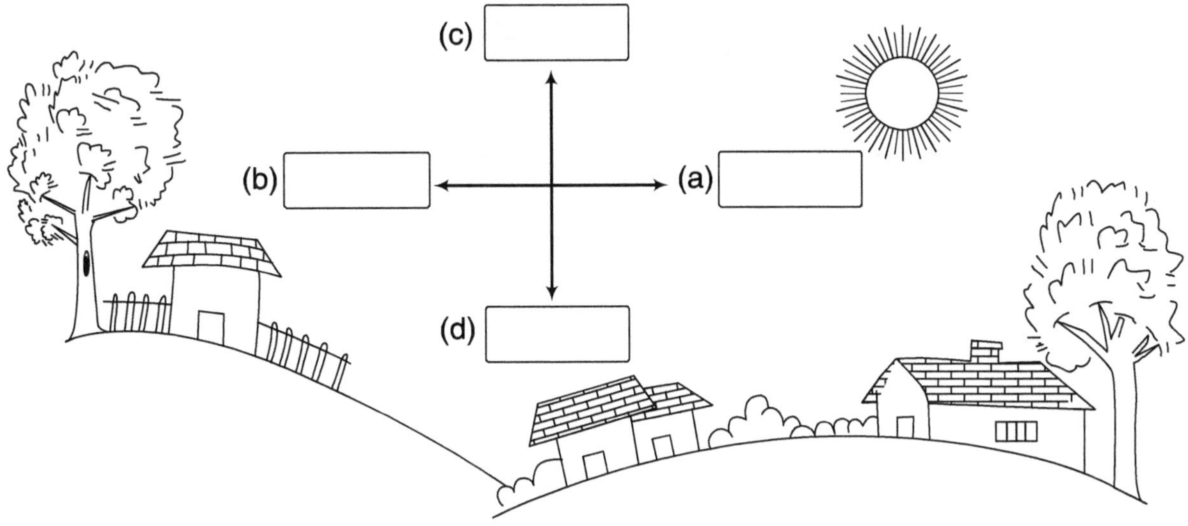

Fun Activity

- Help Lily to reach the mountains, through the maze.

20 Water

- Water is the need of all animals, plants and humans.
- We need water to live.
- Water is very precious.
- We should not waste water.

We need clean water for drinking.

We need water for cooking.

We need water for bathing.

We use water for washing clothes.

We need water for growing plants.

- We get water from rivers, lakes, rain. These are called the sources of water.
- Well and tap are the means of water.

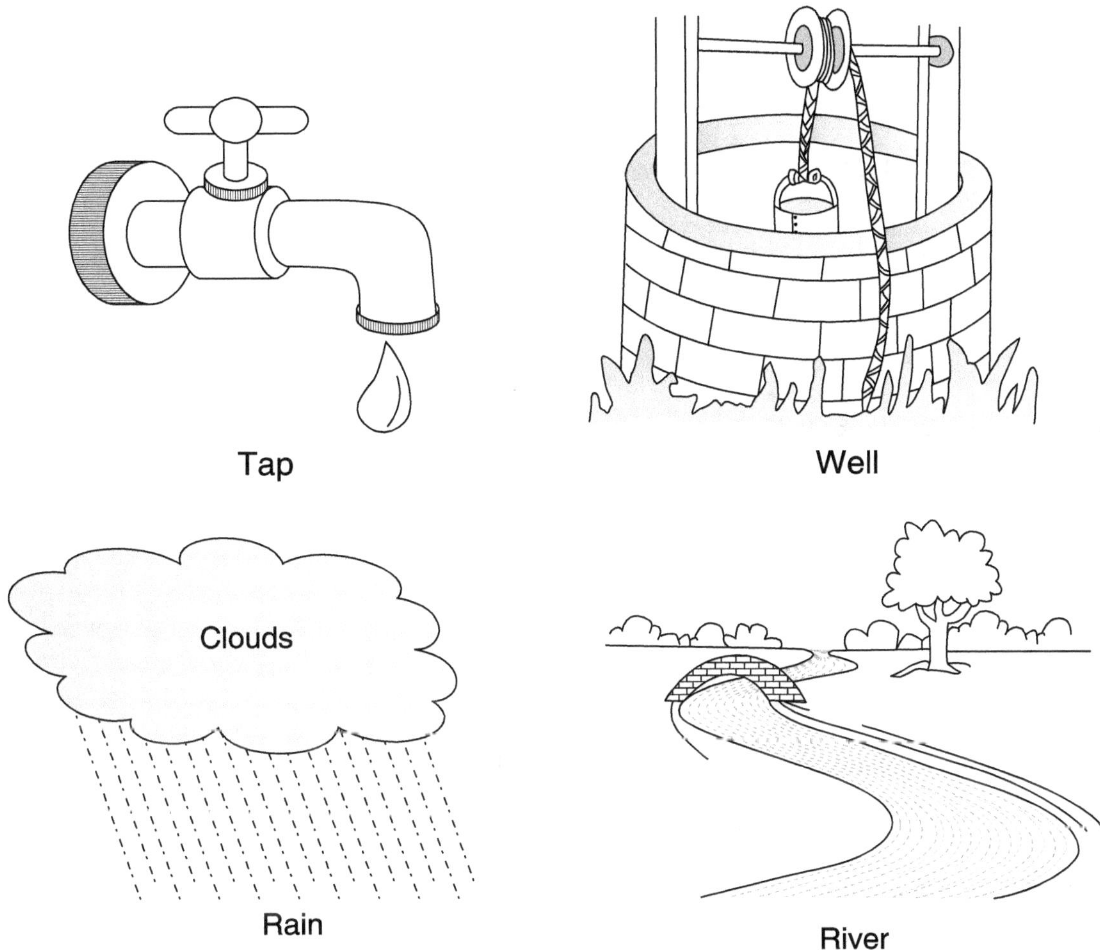

Exercise

1. Fill in the blanks with the help of the words given.

| Precious | Clean | Bathing |

(a) Water is very _____________________________________ .

(b) We use water for _____________________________________ .

(c) We should drink _____________________________ water.

2. Give answers to the following questions.

(a) What are the uses of water?

____

____

(b) Name any two means of water.

____

____

(c) What are the sources of water?

____

____

3. Give your answer in Yes/No.

(a) We should boil water before drinking. _____________

(b) We should not throw garbage in river. _____________

(c) We should keep tap open all the time. _____________

(d) We should not waste water. _____________

4. Arrange the following jumbled words.

(a) A W E T R _______________________________________.

(b) V R E I R _______________________________________.

(c) L E W L _______________________________________.

(d) P T A _______________________________________.

Fun Activity

- Colour the image to complete the fish and let her swim in water.

21

Sky Above Us

- When we go out and look above, we see the sky.
- Sky is blue in the morning.
- Sky turns black during the night.
- Sun rises in the sky in morning and sets in the evening.
- Moon and stars brighten up the sky during the night.
- Rainbow shines in the sky during the rain.

Sun brightens up the sky in the morning

Moon and stars shines in the sky during the night

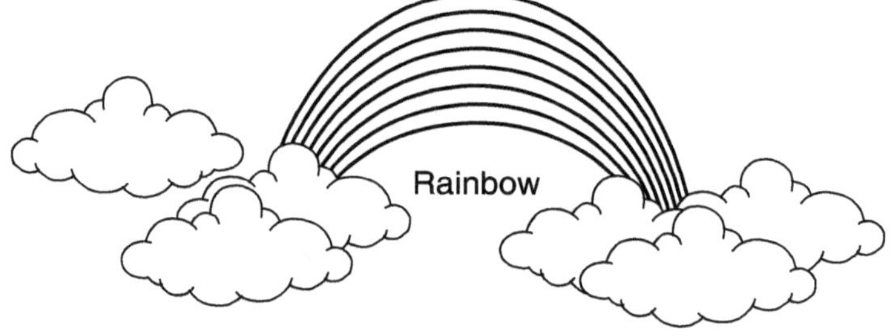

Rainbow has seven colours :
Violet, Indigo, Blue, Green, Yellow, Orange, Red

Sun

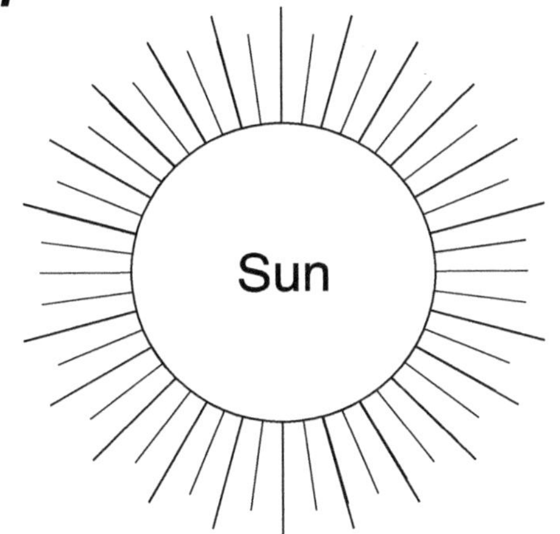

- Sun gives us heat and light.
- Earth moves around the Sun.
- Sun is a ball of burning gases.
- Sun is bigger than Earth.

Air

- Our Earth is surrounded by air.
- Air is necessary for our life.
- We cannot live without air.
- We should keep our air fresh and clean.
- Smoke makes our air dirty.

Seasons

Winter Season

- Winter season is a cold season.
- Snow falls in winter season in hilly areas.
- We wear warm clothes in this season.

Summer Season

- Summer season is a hot season.
- We wear cotton clothes in summers.
- We eat ice-cream in summers.

Rainy Season

- Rainy season is a wet season.
- Rain drops fall from the clouds.
- We carry umbrella to protect ourselves from rain.
- We wear raincoat in the rainy season.

Exercise

1. Fill in the blanks.

Blue   Stars   Smoke   Earth   Rainy

(a) Sky is _________________________ in the morning.

(b) Rainbow appears during the _________________________ season.

(c) During the night _________________________ shine up in the sky.

(d) _________________________ moves around the Sun.

(e) _________________________ makes our air dirty.

2. Match the following.

Category A   **Category B**

(a)   Sun   1. 

(b)   Rain   2. 

(c)   Stars   3. 

(d)   Umbrella   4.

(e)   Raincoat   5. 

3. Complete the following words by filling up the missing letters.

(a) S ___ M ___ ER

(b) R ___ ___ N ___ O ___

(c) ___ I ___ T ___ R

(d) M ___ ___ N

4. Give your answer in Yes/No.

(a) Rainbow has seven colours.

(b) Raincoat protects us from heat.

(c) Sun is a ball of burning gases.

(d) We should keep air clean.

5. Complete the following sentences with help of given words.

wet   warm/hot   cold

(a) Winter is a ________________________season.

(b) Rainy season is a ________________________season.

(c) Summer is a ________________________season.

Fun Activity

- Colour the picture with your favourite colour.

Answers

Chapter 2 About My Body

1. (a) Hair   (b) Eye   (c) Ear   (d) Nose   (e) Lips
2. (a) One   (b) Five   (c) One   (d) Hands
3. (a) Ears   (b) Tongue   (c) Mouth   (d) Eyes
4. (a) Foot   (b) Hand   (c) Eye   (d) Ear   (e) Lips

Chapter 3 My Sense Organs

1. (a) Skin   (b) Eyes   (c) Nose   (d) Tongue
2. Tongue, Nose, Ears, Skin, Eyes
3. (a) Eye   (b) Tongue   (c) Skin   (d) Nose   (e) Ear

Chapter 4 Looking After My Body

2. (a) Yes   (b) Yes   (c) Yes   (d) No
3. (a) Comb   (b) Clean   (c) Brush   (d) Cut

Chapter 5 My Family

1. (e) Grandmother   (f) Father
2. (a) care   (b) playing   (c) cooks   (d) problem
3. (a) My mother is a home maker.

            or

   My mother is a working lady.

Chapter 6 Food To Live

1. (a) Banana   (b) Brinjal   (c) Tomato   (d) Watermelon
   (e) Pineapple   (f) Turnip   (g) Apple
3. (a) Yes   (b) No   (c) Yes

Chapter 7 Need of Clothes

1. (a) Shorts   (b) Frock   (c) Trousers   (d) Skirt   (e) T-shirt
   (f) Gloves   (g) Cap   (h) Shoes
2. (a) CLOTHES (b) SHOES   (c) SOCKS   (d) GLOVES   (d) CAP
3. (a) Head   (b) Gloves   (c) Feet

Chapter 8 Home Sweet Home

1. (a) Pucca House/Kutcha house
   (c) Mud   (d) Bricks   (e) Tall   (f) Kitchen   (g) Bathroom
2. (a) (2)   (b) (1)   (c) (3)
3. (a) KITCHEN   (b) BEDROOM
   (c) DRAWING ROOM   (d) BATH ROOM

Chapter 9 My School

1. (a) Desk   (b) Uniform   (c) Teacher
3. (a) Classroom (b) Books   (c) Playground (d) Black Board
4. (a) (3)   (b) (1)   (c) (2)   (d) (4)
5. (a) Yes   (b) Yes   (c) Yes   (d) Yes

Chapter 10 Good Habits

1. (a) Thank you (b) Pray   (c) Dustbin
2. (a) early   (b) sleep   (c) help   (d) queue
3. (a) Yes   (b) Yes   (c) Yes   (d) No   (e) Yes

Chapter 11 My Neighbourhood

1. (a) DOCTOR   (b) POLICEMAN
   (c) FIREMAN   (d) TAILOR
3. (a) Neighbours   (b) Park   (c) Market
4. (a) Policeman (b) Doctor   (c) Mason   (d) Postman
5. (a) Stitching   (b) Building   (c) Doctor   (d) Thieves

Chapter 12 Festivals

1. (a) 15th August   (b) 26th January   (c) 25th December
2. (a) Holi   (b) Diwali   (c) Eid
3. (a) Food   (b) Republic day   (c) Fire Crackers   (d) Mosque
4. (a) Sewaian   (b) Christmas tree   (c) Mosque   (d) Colour
   (e) Diyas   (f) Sweets   (g) Flowers   (h) Santa Claus
5. (a) Holi is known as the 'Festival of Colours'.
   (b) Sewaian is cooked by people on Eid.
   (c) Santa Claus brings gifts on Christmas.

Chapter 13 The Places of Workship

1. (a) GOD   (b) PRAY   (c) TEMPLE
2. (a) God   (b) Church   (c) One
3. (a) MOSQUE (b) TEMPLE   (c) CHURCH
4. (a) Sikh   (b) Hindu   (c) Muslims   (d) Christian

Chapter 14 Safety Habits

1. (a) Fire   (b) Rush   (c) Strangers
2. (a) Yes   (b) Yes   (c) No   (d) Yes
4. Brush, Shoes, Books

Chapter 15 Means of Transport

1. (a) SHIP   (b) AEROPLANE   (c) BOAT   (d) SCOOTER
2. (a) Scooter   (b) Ship   (c) Bullock Cart   (d) Aeroplane, Train
3. (a) Bus   (b) Air   (c) Ship and Boat
4. (a) Train   (b) Bus   (c) Scooter   (d) Aeroplane
   (e) Boat   (f) Car   (g) Bicycle   (h) Ship

Chapter 16 Road Safety

1. (a) (2)   (b) (1)   (c) (3)
2. (a) Footpath   (b) Run   (c) Zebra Crossing   (d) Down
3. (a) No   (b) Yes   (c) Yes   (d) Yes

Chapter 17 Plant Life

1. (a) Cut   (b) Sunlight   (c) Air   (d) Water
2. (a) Leaf   (b) Fruit   (c) Flower   (d) Seed
3. (a) Big plants are known as trees.   (b) Small plants are know as shrubs.
   (c) We should plant more trees because they gives us food, medicines and cotton.
4. Flower, Leaves, Fruit, Bud and Roots

Chapter 18 Animals Around Us

1. (a) Wings   (b) Fins   (c) Trunk   (d) Horns   (e) Hoof
2. (a) Yes   (b) Yes   (c) Yes   (d) Yes   (e) No
3. (a) (4)   (b) (3)   (c) (5)   (d) (1)   (e) (2)
4. (a) Horns   (b) Tail   (c) Wings   (d) Hooves   (e) Paw

Chapter 19 Our Mother Earth

1. (a) Round   (b) High   (c) Water   (d) Four
   (e) East   (f) West
2. (a) East   (b) West   (c) North   (d) South

Chapter 20 Water

1. (a) Precious   (b) Bathing   (c) Clean

2. (a) Water is used for cooking, bathing, cleaning and watering plants.

(b) Tap and wells are the two means of water.

(c) Rivers, lakes and rainfall are the sources of water.

3. (a) Yes   (b) Yes   (c) No   (d) Yes

4. (a) WATER   (b) RIVER   (c) WELL   (d) TAP

Chapter 21 Sky Above Us

1. (a) Blue   (b) Rainy   (c) Stars   (d) Earth   (e) Smoke

2. (a) 2   (b) 1   (c) 4   (d) 3   (e) 5

3. (a) SUMMER   (b) RAINBOW   (c) WINTER   (d) MOON

4. (a) Yes   (b) No   (c) Yes   (d) Yes

5. (a) Cold   (b) Wet   (c) Warm/Hot

Rough Work

Rough Work

Rough Work

Rough Work

Rough Work